Elephant Snot & Marble Kisses

Courtyard Games Book 2

Minimum Resources …
Maximum Impact

Another book of
Ancient & Modern
Traditional Strategy Games and Puzzles
for Chaplains, Teachers & Children's Workers

Copyright © Gary B Lewis, 2012, 2022

First Published 2012
Second (revised) Edition 2022

Compiled and layout design by Gary Lewis
Photography by Gary Lewis

Website: http://courtyardgames.blogspot.com/

Email: courtyardgames@gmail.com

All rights reserved. No part of this publication may be reproduced, stored in a retrieval system or transmitted in any form by any means, electronic, mechanical, photocopying, recording or otherwise, without the prior permission of the publisher / author.

Elephant Snot & Marble Kisses © Gary B Lewis
Lewis, Gary B 1952 —

Children's Games; Strategy Games; Ancient Games

Print on demand

ISBN: 978-0-646-58314-3

Elephant Snot & Marble Kisses

COURTYARD GAMES BOOK 2

This book is dedicated to all the chaplains and teachers who have not only inspired me to continue being creative, but some of whom have taken up the challenge themselves of building relationships with children through games, setting clear boundaries and safe spaces of grace.

Just like my first book, this book ... **"Elephant Snot & Marble Kisses"**—Courtyard Games book 2, has also been inspired by children and written initially for Primary School Chaplains. However, the resources offered in this book are easily accessible and adaptable for use by anyone working with children—whether they are in children's ministry of any sort: Secondary School Chaplains, Student Wellbeing, beach mission, kid's church, and holiday programs, before/after school care, parents and even grandparents!

Thank you to all the children who keep coming back time after time, year after year. When copies of my first book were presented at both schools' assemblies, there was a sea of hands that went up indicating just how many children had participated in Court Yard Games — or *'Gary Games'* as some kids say. The estimation was over 75% of the schools' population!

I would like to acknowledge kids like Jackson (*name changed*) to whom credit has to be given for the basic concept and development of one the most popular games—*'TOPSY'*.

Once again, thank you to my wife Maree for her enduring patience and constant support and encouragement.

WHY I BELIEVE IN COURT-YARD GAMES

'Court-yard Games' provides a great way for Chaplains and Student Wellbeing Workers for building relationships with a whole range of kids. These kids can come and go as they please ... or stay as long as they like. It's also a great way to spot those isolated kids or the one who just may be out-of-sorts. By staying in the one area each day the Chaplain or Student Wellbeing Worker actually creates a safe space' within an often unfriendly and/or lonely environment for a number of kids who might otherwise wander aimlessly, upset or alone. There have been countless occasions when a student — either known or unknown to me — has sidled up just before the end of lunchtime, sheepishly requesting to having a chat after the bell has gone. The concept of making space for games is really more about *making space for grace* — a place of acceptance.

So rather than just asking or just expecting to be

included in their playground activities or wandering all over the school yard with little direction or intent, let me encourage you to commandeer a space— not too intrusively ... I suggest you don't take over the most popular four-square court for example, or the basketball court or the sandpit! Find a space that is relatively central—avoiding walkways—and make it your own by setting up a new 'Courtyard Game'. By doing this you are inviting the children into this space on your terms. You set the boundaries (visible as well as invisible). You lay out the rules—keeping them as simple and uncomplicated as possible. Now this may sound contrary to the purposes of chaplaincy, but it is actually *you* who determines who plays and when. In my experience, it is a very rare thing for children to have had a fight or any argument during or after any of these games—in fact it has been a wonderful demonstration of *'whosoever will may come'* and play—and come they do! And they come back again and again; and in doing so they are building new friendships across a range of year levels and social groups.

So this collection of games is for you: *to encourage, to inspire and to assist you in your endeavours to build trusting relationships with children in a fun way.*

"Elephant Snot & Marble Kisses" is a cross-section of 20 games that I have either created, discovered, developed or adapted making more use of **minimum resources** ... for even greater **maximum impact**.

The rules and instructions have been kept to a minimum in order to allow you the flexibility for your own interpretation and adaption to suit your own preferences and circumstances.

You may have already discovered that just as sometimes the best fun for a child is an empty cardboard box, and so this second book continues in the same way i.e. with an emphasis on *simplicity* and *making use of what you have*. This is why I firmly believe in finding new ways to use the same materials in new ways, as well as finding ways to utilise recycled / waste materials. If you are in the privileged position to be allocated a budget, then make good use of it. If not, then you will need to do what I have done (and continue to do) and that is to be good at recycling or spending and/or making yourself (which means they are yours to take with you if move on). Remember—***minimum resources … maximum impact!***

Most of these games are competitive but they are all non-physical and non-aggressive. Some of the activities are non-competitive problem solving such as 'Happy Feat' or 'Code Breaker' and others are strategy games such as 'Topsy' or 'Four on the Floor'. And whilst others are simply games of chance such as 'Mouse Hunt' or 'Caterpillar Derby'; some others require patience and skill such as 'Down the Tube', 'Marble Kisses' and 'Elephant Snot' ** which also requires teamwork.

Lastly, some of these Courtyard Games work well for individual participants (sometimes I offer them in one-on-one chat sessions as an icebreaker or as a fun activity after a heavy session); some for partners and some for a group / team. One thing is for sure—they are all fun—especially as you engage with children.

And of course, as you develop your range of games, you will quickly discover that not only will many children come to have their favourites ... so will you.

Have fun!

Gary

In certain cultures this term may be offensive, so please be sensitive to the beliefs and customs of the children with whom you may find yourself working with. Please accept my sincere apology if any offence is taken. The title for this game came about as a spontaneous response from children and teachers when the game was first introduced. As I have essentially chosen to use this title within an Australian context; my suggested alternative name for the game is 'Squishy Tunnel**'.

INSPIRING STORIES

CHECKMATES

One new chaplain was inspired by Courtyard Games at a training session I ran, but was not quite sure what to do. She quickly realised that her school had an outdoor super-sized chess set that no-one used. Finding a group of kids that seemed to be disconnected with others for whatever reason, she taught them how to play chess.

To encourage them in their new game skills she arranged for them to attend and participate in a local chess tournament. Her kids won the tournament! So they were encouraged to go to the district tournament—and they won again! Next were the regional's—and they won again! So then along came the state championships ... and you guessed it ... they won!! They won all because one chaplain was inspired and saw the possibility of connecting with kids through Courtyard Games.

Never underestimate the power of playing Courtyard Games. It positively sets the scene for many *Win-Win* situations.

THINKING OUTSIDE THE SQUARE

Occasionally you will come across a Jackson or a Max.** Kids who will absolutely love the excitement and challenge of every game ... for about two minutes! Then all they want to do is change the rules slightly and make all these suggestions about how to re-arrange the game. You can despair about these kids and quickly lose them, or you can work with them i.e. learn to work with their personalities, their genius and their creativity, and they're yours for keeps. When I found that I could do that i.e. accommodate their incessant '*how about this*' and '*what if we change this*' type of suggestions, I found kids who could actually think outside the square and see something that had never been seen before ... and wallah! A new game concept came into existence! All it needed was some tweaking of framework, rules and design.

The most profound thing I have learned in all this is not the invention of a new game, but the building of a relationship with one of God's precious children, and encouraging them in discovering their own unique place in His world.

** Max's story can be read in Courtyard Games Book 1 ...
http://courtyardgames.blogspot.com/

Inspiring Stories © Gary B Lewis 2012, 2022

TOPSY

Jackson always seemed in to be in trouble. In fact, I'm not even sure why he was referred to me in the first place. Anyway, I do know that whenever he would ask to catch up with the chaplain, it wasn't that he wanted to talk; it was that he just wanted to play a game. But then he was never content with playing any old game, he was always trying out some new idea — which in reality was the same idea he had last time except with improvements! So we went from prototype 1 to prototype 4 and then from Mark I to Mark VI in easy succession—sometimes all within the same session!

The one idea that Jackson persisted with most was that of using the marker-cones in a similar format to the traditional game of Tic Tac To, but he was obsessed about putting the markers on top of each other. One could never quite figure out how to win at this game, because as soon as you thought you had it, Jackson would change the rules again!

TOPSY would be one of the most popular, most competitive, most unpredictable and most challenging. It thrills me immensely to observe little 5-year-old 'Preppies' aka Foundation students undaunted as they take on the challenge of the 6th Graders ... and it is even more special when you see the faces of the 6th

Graders as they try to figure out how a 'Preppie' could have possibly won! After all … this is just like Tic Tac To … isn't it? I guarantee you… you will love its simplicity and you will be enthralled by the challenge of its unpredictability.

Thanks Jackson for your inspiration

Enjoy the games!

Emails :   courtyardgames@gmail.com

Websites :   http://courtyardgames.blogspot.com/

INDEX OF GAMES

	GAME NAME	TYPE	PARTICIPANTS	FORMAT
#1	Tower UP	Game of Skill	2 to 8 players	PAIRS
#2	MARBLE Kisses	Game of Skill	1 player	INDIVIDUAL
#3	TOPSY	Strategy Game	4 players	INDIVIDUAL
#4	Tri-TOPS	Strategy Game	3 players	INDIVIDUAL
#5	MOUSE Hunt	Game of Chance	2 players	INDIVIDUAL
#6	FOUR on the FLOOR	Strategy Game	2 players	INDIVIDUAL
#7	KONO:*5 in a row*	Strategy Game	2 or 4 players	INDIVIDUAL / PAIR
#8	Sir PLUNKETT	Chance / Skill	2 to 4 players	INDIVIDUAL
#9	In the ROUND	Strategy Game	2 plus players	PAIRS
#10	DOWN the TUBE	Chance / Skill	2 to 4 players	INDIVIDUAL
#11	Happy FEAT	Strategy Game	2 to 4 players	TEAM
#12	SPOT On	Chance / Skill	2 to 4 players	INDIVIDUAL
#13	Chopstick SUEY	Game of Skill	1 player	INDIVIDUAL

Indexes & Names of Games © Gary B Lewis 2012 ,2022

#14	Kebab NOODLES	Game of Skill	2 to 8 players	PAIRS
#15	Elephant SNOT**	Game of Skill	2 to 4 players	TEAM
#16	STACK Back	Game of Skill	1 to 8 players	INDIVIDUAL / TEAM
#17	Caterpillar DERBY	Chance / Skill	2 to 4 players	INDIVIDUAL
#18	In the ZONE	Chance / Strategy	2 plus players	INDIVIDUAL / TEAM
#19	Break the CODE	Game of Chance	2 players	INDIVIDUAL
#20	DOMINO DICE Down	Chance / Strategy	3 to 4 players	INDIVIDUAL / TEAM

CROSS REFERENCE INDEX
GAME reference

Equipment Resources as in Book 1 & #2, #3, #4, #5, #6, #7, #8, #9, #11, #13, #18, #18, #19, #20

Strategy Games #3, #4, #6, #7, #9, #11, #18, #19, #20

Partner Games #1, #7, #9, #12, #14, #20

Indexes & Names of Games © Gary B Lewis 2012 ,2022

Hand-eye coordination	#1, #2, #8, #10, #12, #13, #14, #16
Individual Games	#2, #3, #4, #5, #6, #7, #8, #12, #13, #16, #17, #19, #20,
2-Player Games	#1, #5, #9, #10, #14, #18, #19, #20,
3-Player Games	#4,
4-Player Games	#1, #3, #7, #8, #10, #11, #12, #14, #15, #16, #17, #18, #19, #20
Multiple Player Activities	#1, #9, #14, #16, #18,
Teamwork	#11, #15, #16, #18, #19, #20
Ancient Games	#7, #9, #18, #20,
One-off equipment	#1, #2, #5, #8, #10, #14, #15, #16,
Recycled equipment	#1, #2, #3, #6, #7, #9, #10, #11, #12, #13, #14, #15, #17, #18, #19, #20
Dice Games	#17, #18, #19, #20

NOTE: To the best of the author's knowledge this cross reference is accurate but not exhaustive

Indexes & Names of Games © Gary B Lewis 2012 ,2022

1

AIM OF GAME:

- ### COMPETITIVE

To work as a team within the time limit of 2 minutes to land as many discs onto the tower and re-construct a new tower beside the old one.

- ### NON-COMPETITIVE

Players take turns to land as many discs onto the tower and re-construct a new tower beside the old one.

EQUIPMENT REQUIRED:

- 16 coloured bowls / pots (4 of each colour)
- 16 coloured large discs / drum lids (4 of each colour / approx. 250 – 300mm diam

#1

(see diags. #1 & #2)
- 4 small carpet / mat squares
- 24 small rubbers / plastic / wooden discs (approx. 6cm diam.)

  (6 of each colour)
- A timer / stopwatch
- 4 teams of 2 players made up of:
  * 1x DISC THROWER
  * 1 x RE-CONSTRUCTOR

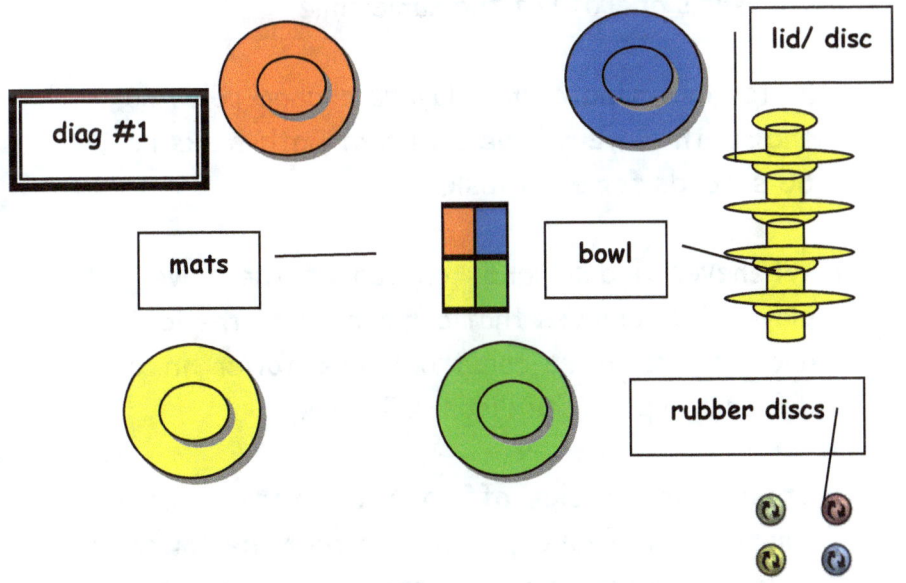

Tower UP © Gary B Lewis 2012, 2022   game #1

#1

RULES OF GAME / HOW TO PLAY:

- ## COMPETITIVE

All teams operate at the same time.

After one minute the players change roles so that both players have a turn at both tasks i.e 60 seconds for each task.

Whenever a disc lands on top of the tower, player #2 removes that component to the left and begins to re-construct the tower in a different spot. (see diags. #3 & #4)

If a disc knocks off one or more tower components of an opponent, so that the tower collapses, then the component(s) is(are) put back in place and that disc is removed from the game - before the game can continue.

Each time player #1 runs out of discs, player

#1

#2 must replenish their supply. Player #1 cannot move off their marked position.

At the end of each timed period, the new tower components are counted and scored.

The winning team scores the highest score in total or alternatively the fastest time to complete both towers.

- ## **NON-COMPETITIVE**

All teams operate in their own time.

Players change roles so that both players have a turn at both tasks without any time limit (depending on how many others are waiting for a turn).

#1

LAYOUT:

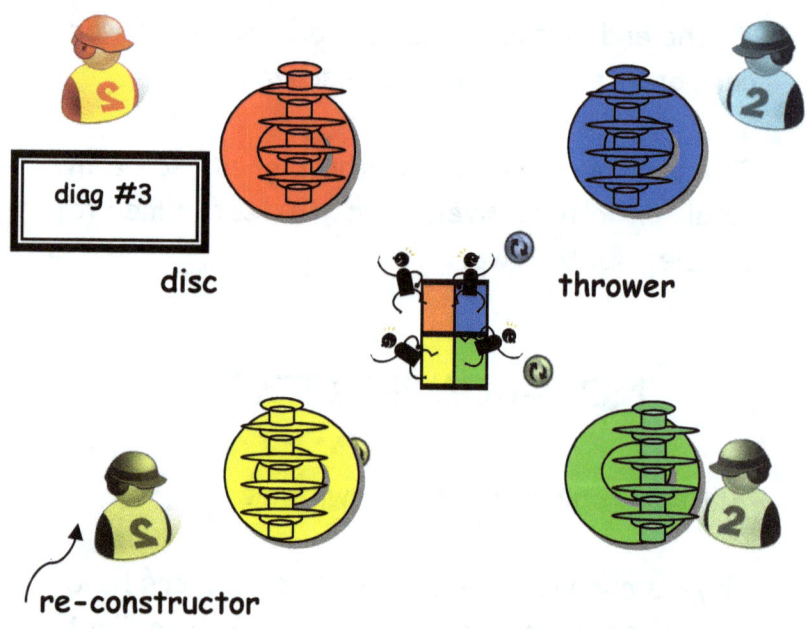

diag #3

disc

thrower

re-constructor

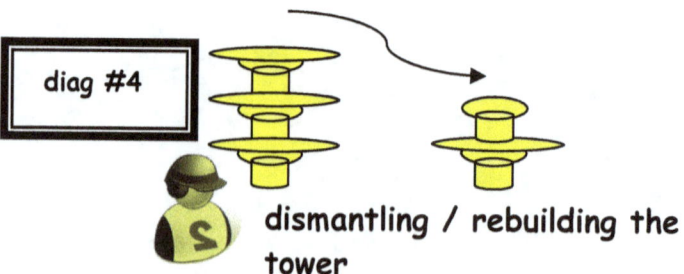

diag #4

dismantling / rebuilding the tower

Tower UP © Gary B Lewis 2012, 2022   game #1

1

Tower UP © Gary B Lewis 2012, 2022   game #1

#2

MARBLE KISSES

© Gary B Lewis

An individual game of skill - a mini version of carpet bowls

AIM OF GAME:

To score points by 'kissing' as many marbles as possible

EQUIPMENT REQUIRED:

- an off-cut / end-of-roll carpet piece is quite inexpensive e.g. outdoor carpet* (see diag. #1)

    *this uses the same piece of carpet green as *'Rainbow Slide'* in Courtyard Games Book 1

- 10 medium-large marbles (various colours)
- 3 'Super Marble' JACKS (commonly known as 'Tom Bowlers') of same colour

#2

- 2 large carpet squares
- 2 bowls / containers
- chalk

DESIGN / LAYOUT:

- set out bowling mat and large carpet squares as shown in diag. #1
- markings on the mat help for placement of 'Super Marble' JACKS and minimum standard for being 'on' the mat
- place 'Super Marble' JACKS on the marked spots (chalk the dots first)
- BOWLER at the bowling end and the KEEPER-RETRIEVER at the other
- the bowl /container is for storing the bowling marbles
- draw a chalk line around the entire game to keep 'other unwanted hands' from interfering

Marble Kisses © Gary B Lewis 2012, 2022   game #2

RULES OF GAME / HOW TO PLAY:

- The bowler bowls their marbles one at a time towards the 'Super Marble' JACK
- If they 'kiss' any marble 'Super Marble' JACK or their own they score points (see score card for details)
- If they 'kiss' and go off the mat they lose 5 points for each of their marbles they knock off the mat
- If they 'kiss' a 'Super Marble' and knock off the 'Super Marble' they can either loose 50 points and the 'Super Marble' JACK is replaced **onto the mat** or they can choose **to not loose** 50 points but the 'Super Marble' JACK remains **off the mat** for the rest of the game
- If they complete the game with all of their marbles & 'Super Marble' JACKS on the mat they score a bonus 50 points
- A bowled marble must reach the 3rd section of the mat to declared 'on' or 'in play'

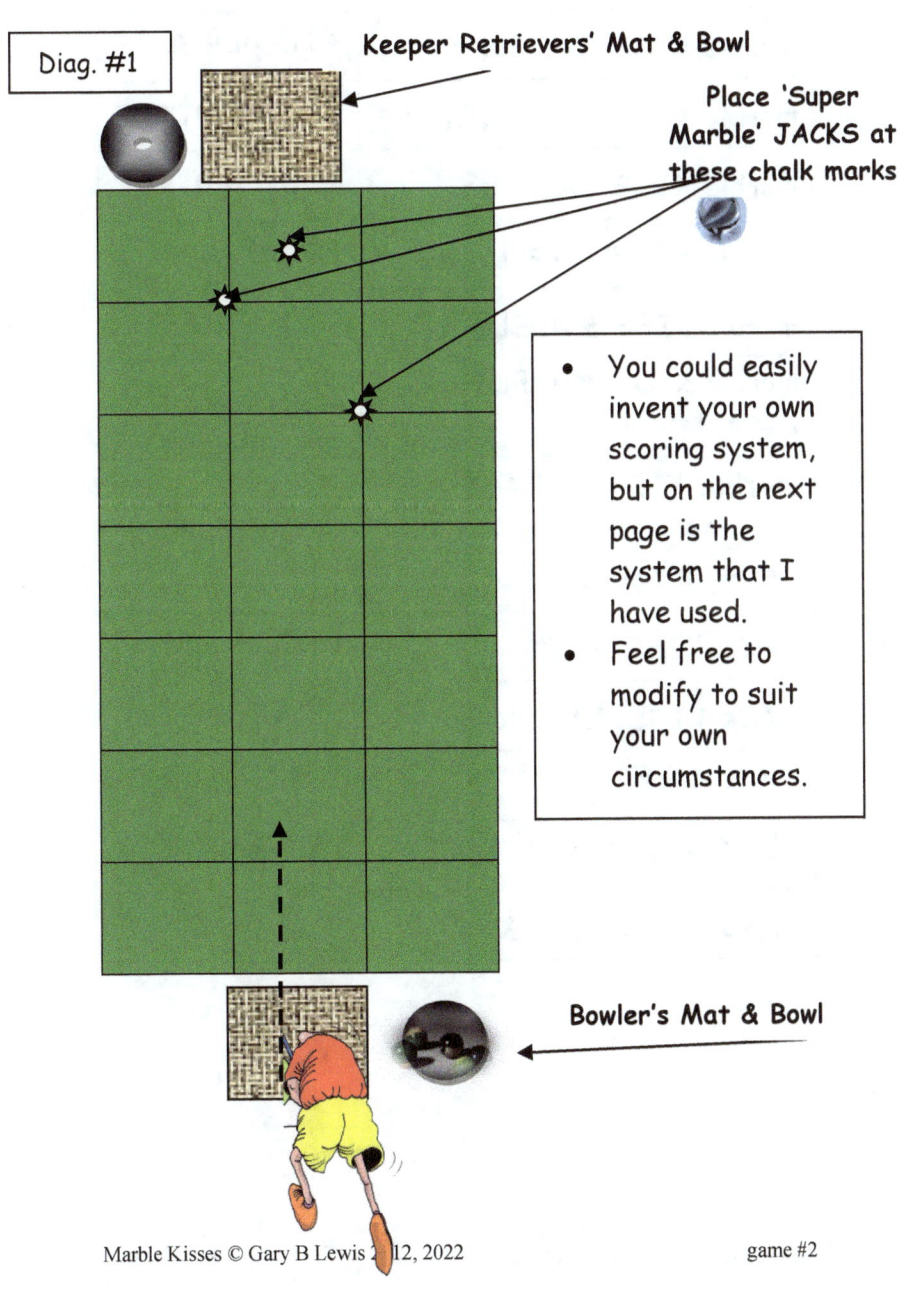

#2

marble KISS JACK x1	+10 points
marble KISS JACK x2	+25 points
marble KISS JACK x3	+50 points
marble KISS MARBLE x1	+5 points
marble KISS MARBLE x2	+15 points
marble KISS MARBLE (more than 3)	+50 points
marble KISS*& JACK KISS** (+5* or 10** per extra)	+20 points
JACK KISS JACK	+100 points
JACK KISS JACK x 3	+200 points
JACK OFF	− 50 points
ALL ON at end of GAME	+50 points
KISS THEN OFF (KTO)	− 5 points

Marble Kisses © Gary B Lewis 2012, 2022

3

TOPSY*

A variation of Naughts & Crosses
Original adaption © Gary B Lewis

A strategy game for 4 players.

AIM OF GAME:

- To get 3 in-a-row as in Yic Yac Yo from Book 1 (see diag. #1)
- A win can be achieved diagonally, vertically or horizontally.

Note: THERE ARE ONLY 5 DIRECTIONAL WAYS TO WIN IN THIS GAME (see diag. #1)

*Make sure you read Jackson's story and the creation of 'TOPSY' at the end of these instructions

EQUIPMENT REQUIRED:

- grid-layout (see diag. #1)
    - either chalk drawn or vinyl circles (approx. 300mm diam.)
    - optional extra made of carpet squares

3

(approx. 300mm x 300mm sq.)
- rubber / plastic markers / discs / cones** (4 colours / 6 each)

** *Cones work much better because of their stack-ability*

DESIGN & LAYOUT:

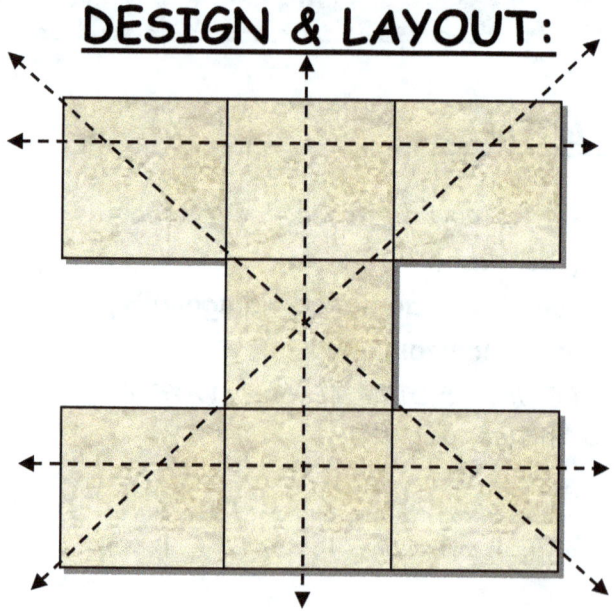

diag #1

TOPSY © Gary B Lewis 2012, 2022   game #3

#3

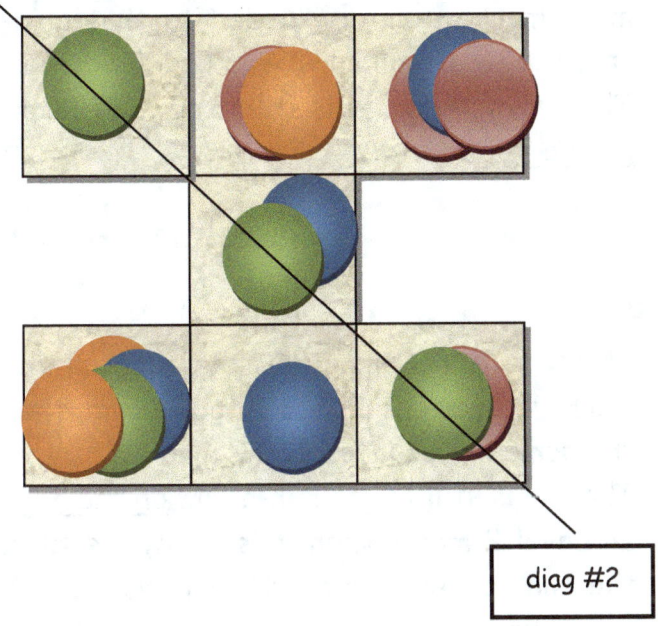

diag #2

HOW TO PLAY:

LEVEL 1

- Players take turns to place their markers on the grid.
- They can place their marker on 'top' of another colour but <u>not</u> immediately 'topping' their own colour. (see diag. #2 / photo #1)
- Once there are 4 topped on any <u>one</u> space, then "*TOPS*" is declared – meaning that no

#3

more markers can be added to that grid-space.
- The aim of the game is still to get 3 in-a-row <u>on the 'top'</u>.

(see diag. #2 / photo #2)

LEVEL 2

- If there is no winner by the time all the marker-cones are placed onto the grid, then the game moves into Level 2 mode.
- The aim is still to get 3 in-a-row <u>on the 'top'</u>.
- In Level 2 mode when it is a player's turn, the can remove one of their marker-cones from the bottom of a stack from anywhere on the grid.
    - **NOTE: the marker-cone that is removed MUST be at the bottom – even if it is by itself on a grid-space it is still counted as bottom.**
- The removed marker-cone can now be placed anywhere on the grid except on a "*TOPS*" space.

3

- **NOTE:** *the fun and intrigue about this game is that the strategy for winning and blocking is the opposite of Naughts and Crosses.*
- *Instead of blocking your opponent's winning opportunity by going onto a blank space ... you need to go on 'top' of them.*
- *Children will quickly learn that their chances of winning are far better by being on top of a "TOPS" stack.*

3

For another variation of this game check out TRI-TOPS next page

Photos #1 & #2

TOPSY © Gary B Lewis 2012, 2022

#5

AIM OF GAME:

- To get 3 in-a-row as in Yic Yac Yo from Book 1 (see diag. #1)
- A win can be achieved diagonally, vertically or horizontally.

Note: THERE ARE ONLY 4 DIRECTIONAL WAYS TO WIN IN THIS GAME (see diag. #1)

*Make sure you read Jackson's story and the creation of 'TOPSY' at the end of these instructions

EQUIPMENT REQUIRED:

- grid-layout (see diag. #1)
  - ❖ either chalk drawn or vinyl circles (approx. 300mm diam.)
  - ❖ optional extra made of carpet squares

#5

(approx. 300mm x 300mm sq.)
- rubber / plastic markers / discs / cones** (3 colours / 5 each)
    - ** *Cones work much better because of their stack-ability*

DESIGN & LAYOUT:

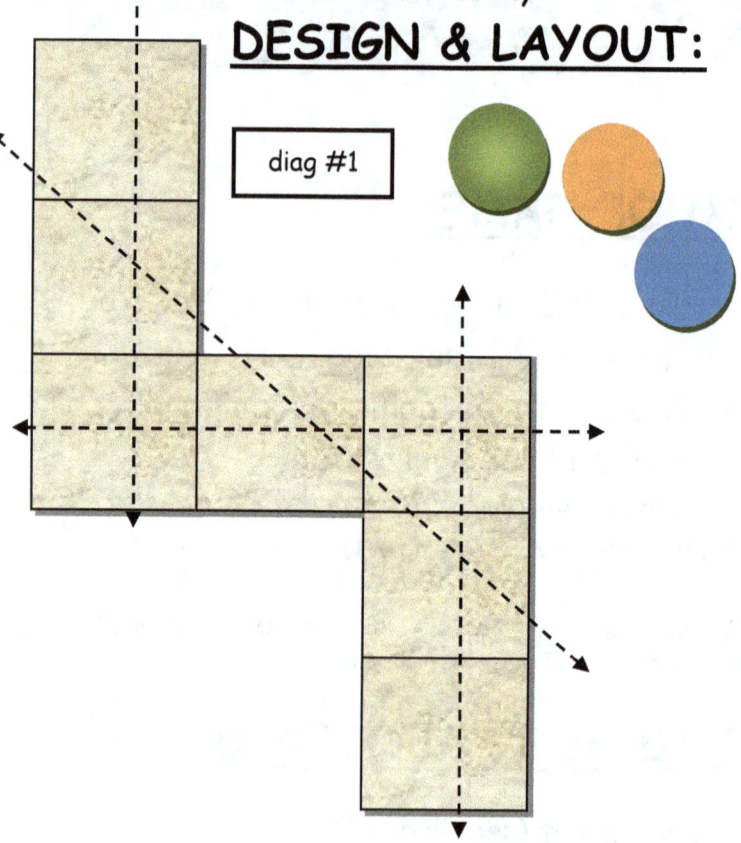

diag #1

Mouse Hunt © Gary B Lewis 2012, 2022

#5

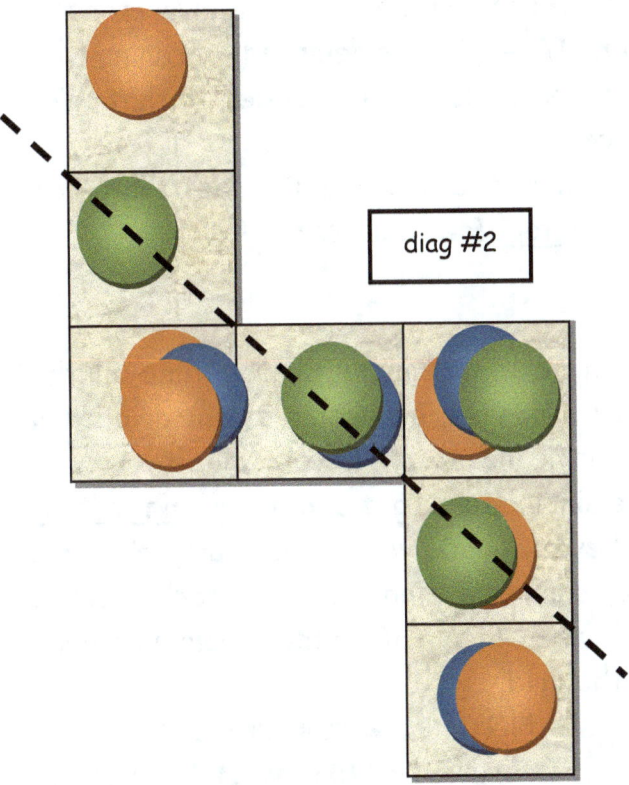

diag #2

HOW TO PLAY:

LEVEL 1

- Players take turns to place their markers on the grid.
- They can place their marker on 'top' of another colour except not immediately

'topping' their own colour. (see diag. #2)
- Once there are 3 topped on anyone space, then "*TRI-TOPS*" is declared – meaning that no more markers can be added to that grid-space.
- The aim of the game is still to get 3 in-a-row <u>on the 'top'</u>. (see diag. #2)

LEVEL 2

- If there is no winner by the time all the marker-cones are placed onto the grid, then the game moves into Level 2 mode.
- The aim is still to get 3 in-a-row <u>on the 'top'</u>.
- In Level 2 mode when it is a player's turn, they can remove one of their marker-cones from the bottom of a stack from anywhere on the grid.
    - **NOTE: the marker-cone that is removed MUST be at the bottom – even if it is by itself on a grid-space it is still counted as bottom.**
- The removed marker-cone can now be placed anywhere on the grid except on a "*TRI-TOPS*" space.

#5

- *NOTE: the fun and intrigue about this game is that the strategy for winning and blocking is the opposite of Naughts and Crosses.*
- *Instead of blocking your opponent's winning opportunity by going onto a blank space ... you need to go on 'top' of them.*
- *Children will quickly learn that their chances of winning are far better by being on top of a "TRI-TOPS" stack.*

Make sure you check out the original version of "TOPSY" (game #3) and read Jackson's story

#5

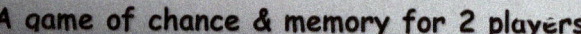

AIM OF GAME:

- To find 'mice' hidden underneath pots. The winner finds the most mice.

EQUIPMENT REQUIRED:

- 4x4 grid — either chalk drawn or made of 16 carpet squares (approx. 300mm) (see diag. #1)
- 8 vinyl circles (approx. 300mm diam.) (see diag. #1)

Mouse Hunt © Gary B Lewis 2012, 2022

#5

- 16 pots / buckets either same / different colours (preferably without holes in the bottom)
- Laminated letters A-B-C-D
- Laminated numbers 1-2-3-4
- 6 'MOUSE' mascots*

These can be bought cheaply from $2 shops or pet stores

DESIGN & LAYOUT:

- Set up the grid as shown with LETTER-NUMBER grid-co-ordinates (see diag. #1) Grid size = approx. 2100mm x 2100mm
- Place the 16 pots up-side-down on the grid-spaces
- Hide 5 of the 'MOUSE' mascots underneath different pots (one-pot-one-mouse)
- Place the last 'MOUSE' mascot on top of any of the up-side-down pots (see diag. #1)

#5

RETRIEVER-MOUSE GATHERER

INSTRUCTOR-MOUSE HUNTER

RULES OF GAME:

- Players decide who goes first – only THE RETRIEVER-MOUSE GATHERER is permitted on the grid. The INSTRUCTOR-MOUSE HUNTER stands outside to give instructions for the co-ordinates e.g B2 or C3 etc
- Player #1 as INSTRUCTOR-MOUSE HUNTER tries to find a mouse by instructing Player #2 as RETRIEVER-MOUSE GATHERER which pot to turn right-side-up.
    - If there is a mouse underneath the pot then the mouse belongs to Player #1 and the mouse is given to Player #1. Then it is Player #2's turn to instruct Player #1
    - If there is no mouse underneath the pot then Player #1 has a free turn
- Each time a mouse is found it is given to the current INSTRUCTOR-MOUSE HUNTER
- Play continues in this format of Player #1 and Player #2 inter-changing positions of being INSTRUCTOR-MOUSE HUNTER & RETRIEVER-MOUSE GATHERER

#5

- A free turn is given until each time an empty pot is up-turned only until there is <u>one mouse left</u> under the pots. When there is only one mouse left in the game – <u>there are NO MORE FREE TURNS</u>
- If a player - *INSTRUCTOR-MOUSE HUNTER* - chooses the pot with the 'mouse on top' and it has a mouse underneath, they get to keep both mice. However if there is no mouse underneath then the 'mouse on top' is given away to the *RETRIEVER-MOUSE GATHERER player*
- At the end of the game the player with the most 'MOUSE' mascots wins or it is a draw with both players scoring the same (3 mice each)

6

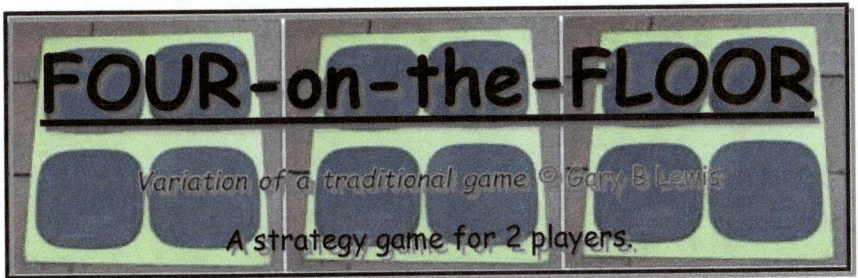

AIM OF GAME:

To get 4 of your markers in a row vertically, horizontally or diagonally

MATERIALS REQUIRED:

<u>NOTE</u>: This game uses the same boards as the 'Coloured Boundaries' game in Courtyard Games Book 1.
- MDF board approx. 6mm thick. Cut 6 sections of 400 x 450mm.
  Paint or stick on four 'divided spaces'

  (see photo / diag. #1)
- Each player requires 8 markers
  16 markers ... 8 x 2 colours

6

LAYOUT:

diag. #1

Four on the Floor © Gary B Lewis 2012, 2022

game #6

6

HOW TO PLAY:

LEVEL 1:
Set up the board as shown in diag. #1

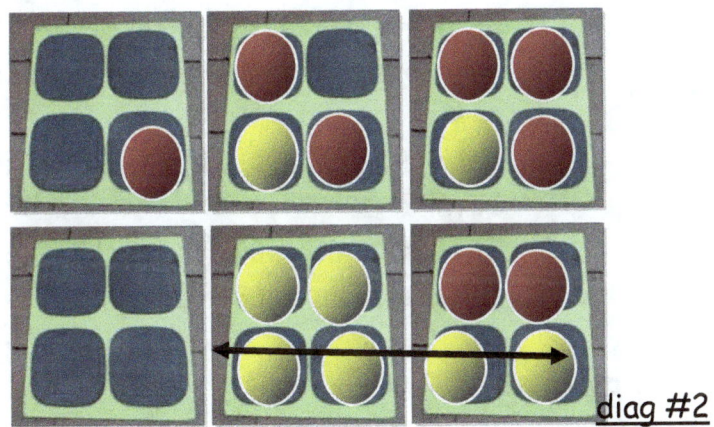

diag #2

- Players take turns to place their markers on the grid
- Players aim to line up 4 of their markers vertically, horizontally or diagonally (see diag. #2)
- Only one *marker* in each grid-space at a time
- If there is no winner by the time all markers are down, then the game moves onto Level 2

Four on the Floor © Gary B Lewis 2012, 2022

6

LEVEL 2:
- When there is no winner in Level 1, then move into Level 2 mode where:
    - Players take turns in removing one of their own markers and moving it onto an empty grid-space.
    - Play continues in order to get 4 in a row
    - Each player gets **only 4 moves** in Level 2.
    - If there is no winner in Level 2, then the game moves onto Level 3

LEVEL 3:
- When there is no winner in Level 2, then move into Level 3 mode where:
    - Players take turns moving / sliding one section of the grid to the left or right / up or down
      (see diags. #3 & #4)
    - Play continues in order to get 4 in a row
    - Each player can **only move up to 3** grid-sections in Level 3.
    - If there is no winner in Level 3, then the game moves onto Level 4

Four on the Floor © Gary B Lewis 2012, 2022

6

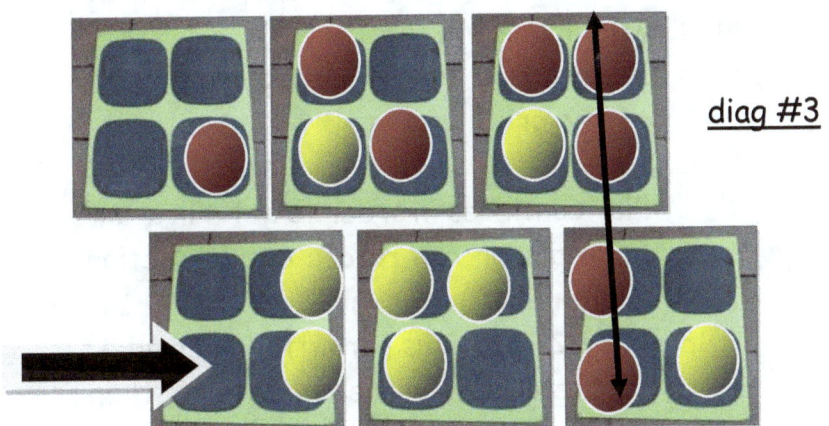

diag #3

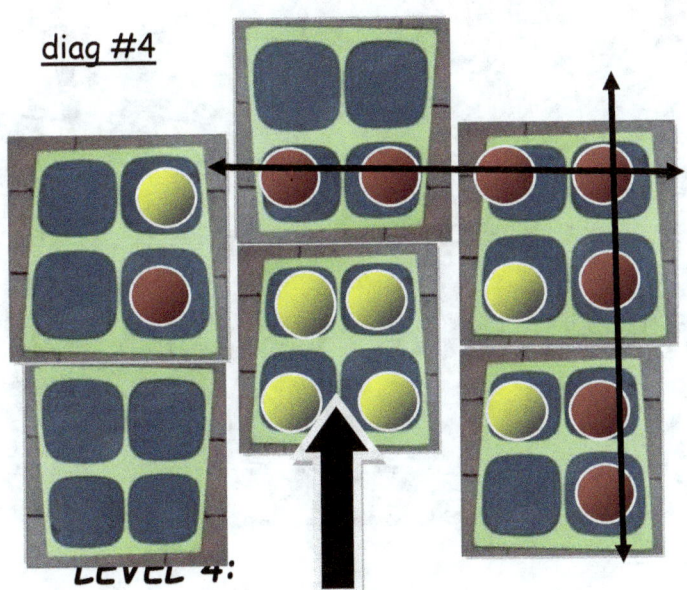

diag #4

LEVEL 4:

Four on the Floor © Gary B Lewis 2012, 2022

6

- When there is no winner in Level 3, then move into Level 4 mode where:
    - Players take turns rotating one section of the grid

        (see diag. #5)
    - Play continues in order to get 4 in a row
    - Each player can rotate a grid-section (90° or 180°) in Level 4
    - **Only 2 rotations** permitted in Level 4
    - If there is no winner in Level 4, then the game is declared a draw!

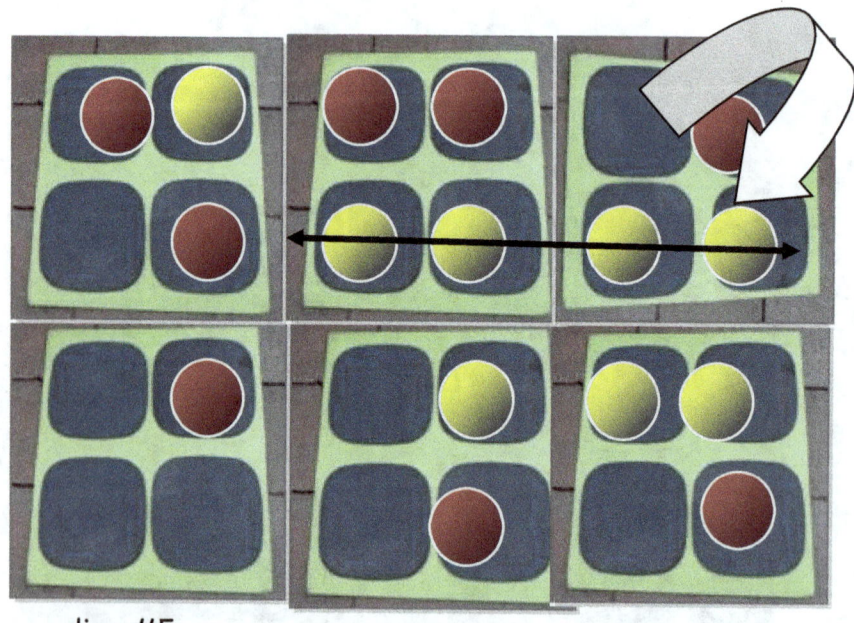

diag #5

Four on the Floor © Gary B Lewis 2012, 2022

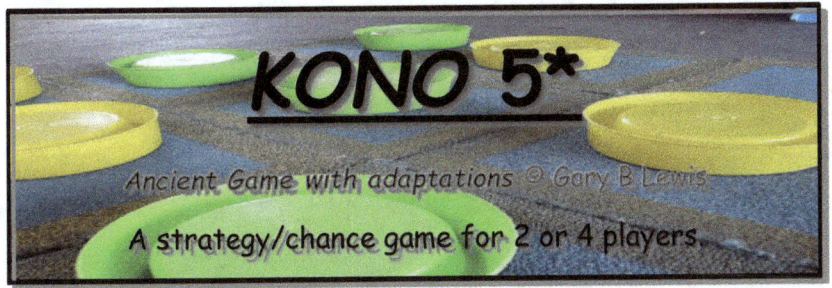

*A variation of KONO:4 IN-A-ROW - Book 1

AIM OF GAME:

To move all of your MEN' to the opposite side of the board first — only moving DIAGONALLY.

* **NOTE**: This game is also very similar to Checkers / Draughts

MATERIALS REQUIRED:

- 5 X 6 grid
- 14 markers
    - 7 x 2 colour markers
- grid as shown (see diag. #1)
- grid squares from vinyl or carpet

Kono: 5 in-a-row © Gay B Lewis 2012, 2022

#7

- lines can be drawn with chalk or
- gaffer/masking tape if inside

diag. #1

LAYOUT:

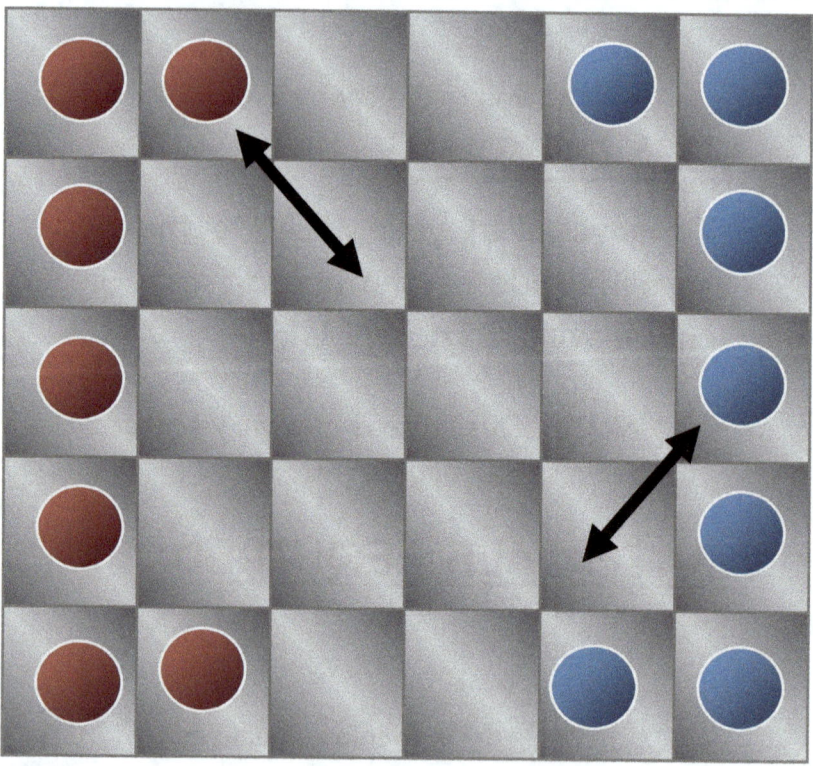

Kono: 5 in-a-row © Gay B Lewis 2012, 2022

#7

HOW TO PLAY:

Set up the board as shown in diag. #1

* Game can be played with either two or four players operating as two teams
  - ❖ Encourage 'talking' with partner
* Players move <u>one grid-space at a time</u> ... *only diagonally*
* Players can move forwards and backwards diagonally
* No horizontal or vertical moves
* JUMPING is PERMITTED ... but not until you have at least 2 MEN 'home'.
  - ❖ Diagonal jumps only – over any coloured marker
  - ❖ No capturing of opponent's MEN
* Only one MAN in each grid-space at a time

* REMEMBER: **YOU CAN ONLY WIN BY GETTING ALL YOUR MEN ONTO THE OTHER SIDE OF BOARD IN THE SAME PATTERN**

Kono: 5 in-a-row © Gay B Lewis 2012, 2022

#7

Check out 'KONO :4 IN-A-ROW' & 'GIANT CHECKERS' in COURTYARD GAMES BOOK 1.

Kono: 5 in-a-row © Gay B Lewis 2012, 2022

10

AIM OF GAME:

The aim of 'SIR PLUNKETT' is to score as many points as possible by pulling the giant sticks out of the holes before all the balls fall to the bottom of the tub.

MATERIALS REQUIRED:

This game makes use of the GIANT PICK-UP STICKS from Courtyard Games Book 1. (See book 1 for how to make)

10

- 24 coloured sticks approx. 600 mm in length – 6 x 4 colours
  - use dowel or bamboo garden stakes
- 2 extra sticks – one white / one black
- 4 coloured arm bands to identify players
- 1 x square plastic storage tub with holes drilled into the sides
- 2 or 3 dozen light plastic balls
- 1 x empty cloth bag (storage for plastic balls) as lucky dip
- Chalk
- Pre-drill holes large enough to poke the sticks through

LAYOUT:

- Set up the tub, sticks and balls as shown in photos #1-3
- Outline the playing area with chalk – e.g. 300mm to 450mm around the tub. Only one player at a time can be in the playing area.

10

HOW TO PLAY:

Establish the order of play. When it is their turn, each player has a lucky dip in the bag which has one of each of the coloured balls. The ball that they pull out of the bag indicates which coloured stick they have to try to carefully slide out of the tub through the holes, without causing any balls to fall through to the bottom.

If the coloured '*lucky dip*' *ball* matches the colour of their own colour band, then they can double the points scored for that turn e.g. 10 points – once they have removed the coloured stick from the tub.

If the colour of the lucky dip ball is a different colour to their colour band then only 5 points are scored - once they have removed the coloured stick from the tub.

10

If they successfully remove the stick from the tub without any balls dropping to the bottom, then they can either score double points or have a free turn.

Whatever, they decide to do, whenever a ball or balls fall to the bottom of the tub, it is the next player's turn. If the player has already moved a stick, then they must continue to remove it as they end their turn.

SAFETY RULE:

Encourage each player to place their 'captured' sticks on the ground in front of them whilst they await their next turn. Otherwise they may have to lose points for unsafe behaviour or if their sticks fall into the playing area.

10

If a player pulls out a coloured ball that has no corresponding colour sticks left in the game, then they must remove a black or white stick for only 2 points each.

Play continues until all the balls have fallen to the bottom of the tub – even though there still might be a dozen sticks left.

> NOTE: Add up each player's scores as they each complete their turns and expect that they will remember – otherwise keep a score card handy.

The most frustrating thing about this game is the re-setting up for the next round of players. However, chaos can be avoided by allocating certain children specific roles to carry out e.g.
- collect the balls and place them in the bag
- have 2 or 3 students responsible for repositioning the sticks through the holes – never force them through

10

- allow one student to carefully pour the balls back into the tub on top of the sticks – keeping aside one of each colour for the lucky dip bag.
    - NOTE: do not be too concerned that when you tip out the balls on top of the sticks ... that some will no doubt automatically fall through to the bottom.

Photos
#1 - #3

10

AIM OF GAME:

The same as for YIC YAC YO (Book 1). Each player tries to place their markers 3 in a row.

This 'IN-THE-ROUND' version simply allows you to set up a series of games all being played at the same time in *Round Robin* style. The winner of each game moves onto the next grid and plays the <u>non-winner</u> (loser) of the previous game.

10

The ultimate aim is to establish the CHAMPION YIC YAC YO player on the CHAMPION'S GRID / WINNER'S CIRCLE.

MATERIALS REQUIRED:

<u>NOTE</u>: the amount of equipment required will be determined by how many grids you decide to set up e.g. if you are using 6 grids then multiply the number of carpet squares & markers by 6.
So for a 6-grid game you will need 54 squares & 72 markers.

If you are ambitious you can reproduce large X's & O's (at the risk of them being used as Frisbees or Ninja Spikes!!!) Recommended that you use rubber / plastic markers.

Set up 3 x 3 grid using either rubber-backed carpet or vinyl cut-outs <u>circles are better</u> (approx. 300mm diam.) See diag. #1
12 discs / markers — 6 of each colour

- If playing on asphalt / concrete you could use <u>chalk</u> to draw lines ahead of time.

Down the Tube © Gary B Lewis 2012, 2022

10

- If playing on floorboards / carpet then use <u>masking tape</u>.

LAYOUT:

Before setting up you need to decide how many grids you will require. One clue is to go by the regular number of children attending Courtyard Games activities.

diag. 1

My suggestion is to determine the number of grids by your own capacity i.e. of how many games you can possibly oversee at any one time.

My suggestion would be a maximum of 6 grids running simultaneously lay out in an arch. This seems to conveniently make better use of restricted space. (see diag. #2)

Down the Tube © Gary B Lewis 2012, 2022

10

The last grid can be called 'THE WINNER'S GRID' or 'THE CHAMPION'S CIRCLE' – come up with your own title.

HOW TO PLAY:

You can actually start the 'IN-THE-ROUND' with just the first grid game playing – best out of 3 games; or you can start all grids playing at the same time. It really does not matter.

The best way to decide who goes first <u>at the start of every game</u> is to do 'Rock-Paper-Scissors', then alternate going first. This will save a lot of arguments. Alternatively you can have the 'non-winner' (the one who stayed at the

10

grid) to start the first game then take turns as to who goes first until the next sequence of games.

If there is no winner at the end of the third game, you can either allow them to play one more game or get them to do 'Rock-Paper-Scissors' again to determine the winner who moves on to the next grid.

At the last grid — *the WINNER'S GRID or the CHAMPION'S CIRCLE* — the winner stays and the loser is out. The final non-winner can re-enter the game back at grid one if they want to. (see diag. #2)

Just be aware that some younger children cannot last the distance of playing so many games in a row, and so they may wish to pull out after one or two games. If so, just quickly pull in the 'next' player waiting their turn to get in.

10

If you establish the ground rules early and simply, you will have very few problems running this 'IN-THE-ROUND' activity. The kids will love it.

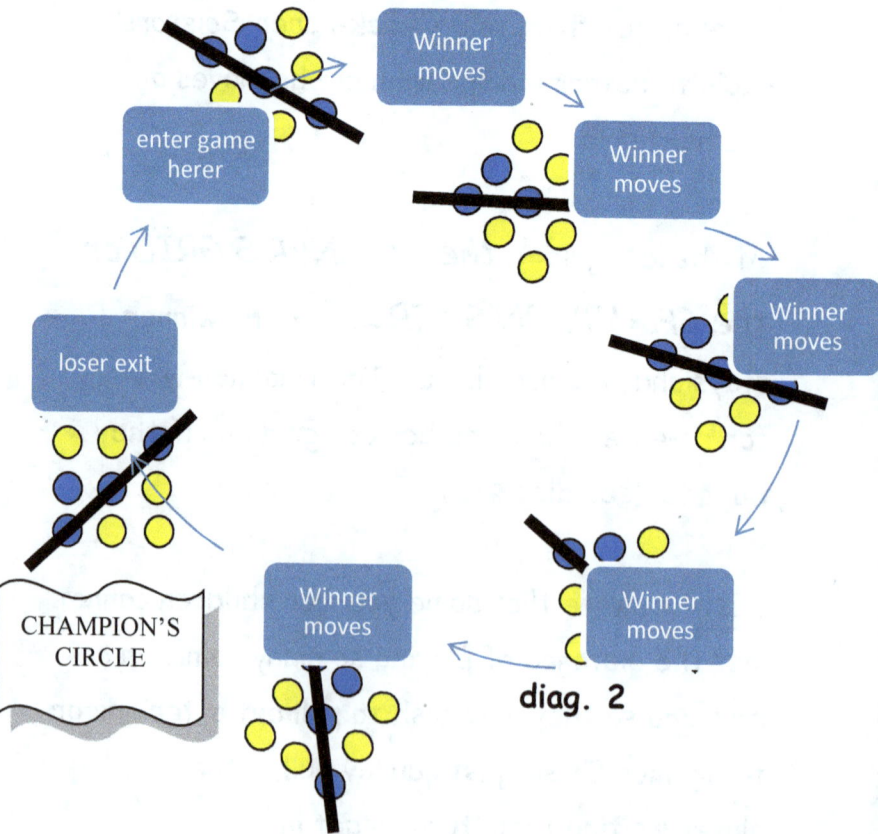

diag. 2

10

A strategy / chance & game of skill for 3-4 players.

AIM OF GAME:

The aim of 'DOWN THE TUBE' is threefold:

1. For the 'MUFFIN MAN' (trapper) to trap as many marbles as possible
2. For the 'DROPPER' to drop their marbles down the tube and not be captured
3. For the 'CUPPA' to catch as many marbles as possible in their cup before going off the edge.

10

MATERIALS REQUIRED:

- A large cardboard tube or PVC pipe approx. 1 metre in length & approx. 100-120mm diam.
- A 1500mm length of flexible clear plastic tubing approx. 30-40mm in diameter. This will need to be cut to length to suit the length of your large TUBE
- A vinyl or carpet piece approx. 600mm x 300mm
- 2 carpet squares approx. 300mm sq
- A light soft plastic cup
- A safety ear-muff (called 'THE MUFFIN') removed from a set of safety ear-muffs to be used to trap the marbles.
- A set of about 10 marbles – different colours preferably as this will challenge the MUFFIN MAN'S reflexes more so (or not!)

To make the 'TUBE' simply drill / cut some holes about the size of the diameter of your clear plastic tubing towards the top, middle and bottom of your large TUBE. Then carefully weave the plastic tubing from the top down through the TUBE in & out of the middle and back out the bottom.

NOTE: Be careful not to crunch the tubing too

10

tight as the marbles will not roll freely down.

The TUBE will probably not stand upright by itself and so an extra pair of hands (yours or another player – the 'HOLDER') will be required to keep the TUBE steady and facing in the correct direction. By slightly tilting the TUBE backwards you are able to slow down the marble's speed just a little.

LAYOUT:

- Set out the playing area as shown in diag. #1
- At one of the playing area the 'CUPPA' person sits on the carpet square holding the cup on its edge. Their job is to collect all the marbles that are missed by the 'MUFFIN MAN'.
- The 'DROPPER' person is at the other end of the playing area. The job is to call out "*DROP!*" each time they drop a marble down the TUBE.
- The 'HOLDER' stands to the side of the 'DROPPER'.
- The 'MUFFIN MAN' kneels on the other carpet square to the right of the 'DROPPER'

10

(if they are right-handed or to the left if they are left-handed)

HOW TO PLAY:

This game is extremely popular with kids of all ages, because as the MUFFIN MAN you get to test your reflex skills. It is a great leveller of superiority and arrogance, as well as a great opportunity for building self-esteem and encouragement.

1. If you are using a '**holder**', then you 4 positions that every person gets to have a shot at. Every position contributes to the game.
2. With everyone in position and ready the 'DROPPER' calls out "*DROP!*" as they release their marbles one-at-a-time, and waiting for the other players to be ready for the next

10

drop.

3. The 'MUFFIN MAN' tries to trap the dropped marble before it heads off towards the 'CUPPA'. Have a restricted area with about 200mm from the base of the TUBE that the 'MUFFIN MAN' is not allowed to trap.

4. The 'MUFFIN MAN' must have their MUFFIN off the ground — not resting on the ground — in order to trap the marbles i.e. marbles are trapped with a *whack* not a *lay-down-tilt* of the MUFFIN.

5. The 'CUPPA' person's job is to collect all the marbles that are missed by the 'MUFFIN MAN'. If 'CUPPA' person lines up their cup correctly, then the marbles should roll straight in - but otherwise they will have to go chase them. Marbles that belong to the 'CUPPA' are placed on the corner of their mat so that they are

10

able to move their cup about freely.

6. The winner is the one who beats their own best score or the one who gets the highest marbles trapped with the MUFFIN.
7. Once all the marbles have been dropped rotate the players until all 4 have had their turn at every position.

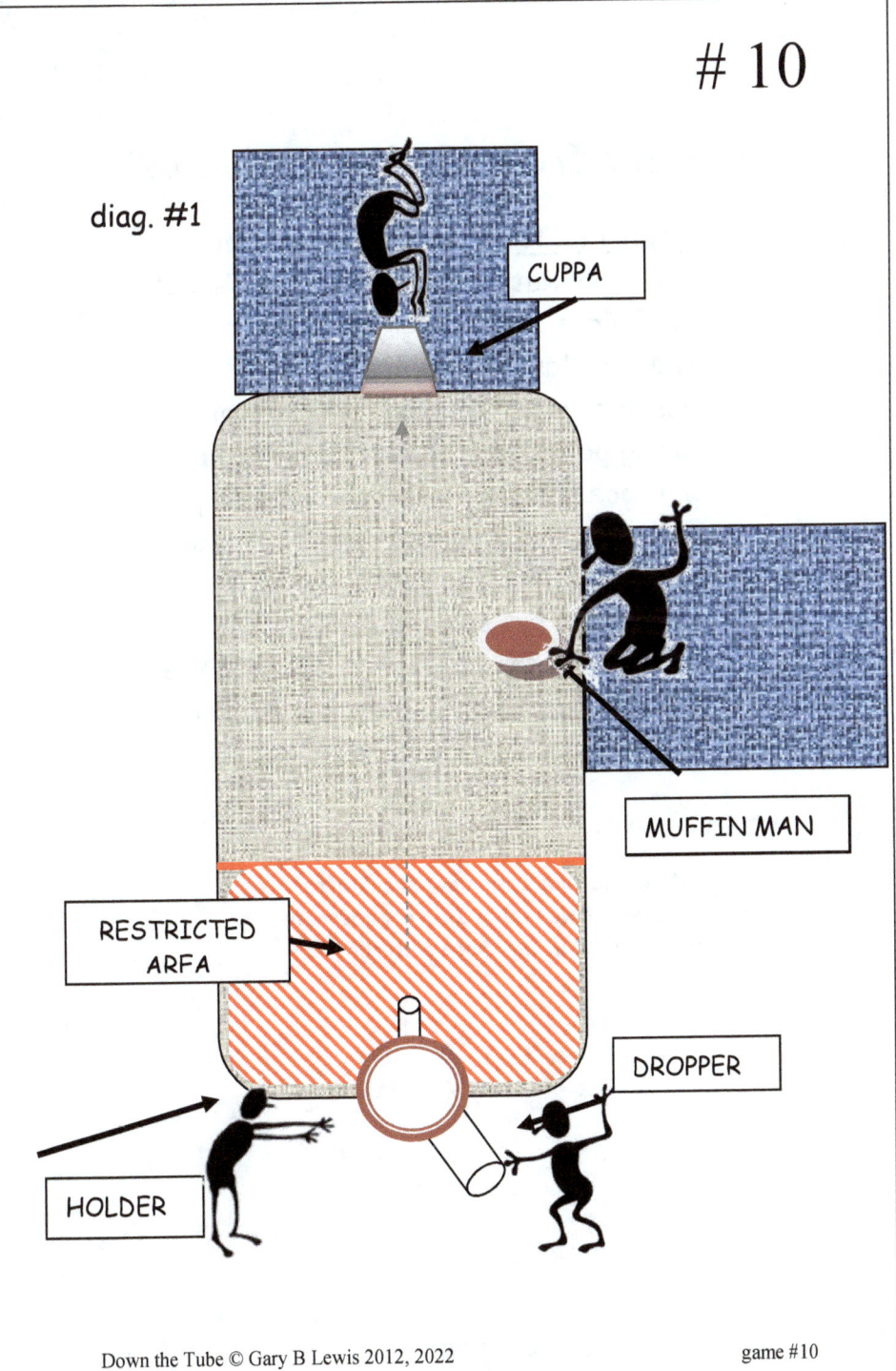

10

Comment from another enthusiast ...

<u>'Down the Tube'</u> seems very similar to "*Bash the Rat*", a game that is played at the Tolmie Sports (very significant event in Mansfield Shire). A "mad" Irishman runs this game which involves rolling potatoes (the rats) down a pipe that goes through a wooden box, so you can't see the progress of the rat. As it comes out onto the table, the person playing has to use a piece of rubber tubing to bash it before it rolls off the table. No scoring, just the pure silliness of bashing a bit of potato**.

(Thanks Sue)

** Let it be said that I too have seen Jaffas being smashed as well ... but I do not advocate food being wasted in any shape or form!

11

A cooperative strategy game of memory for 2 or more players

AIM OF GAME:

To get your 'Happy Feat' mascot safely via the secret path across the obstacle course grid by using memory skills. (see diag. #1)

EQUIPMENT REQUIRED:

- 7x7 grid
  - ❖ either chalk drawn or made of carpet squares (approx. 300mm) (see diag. #1)
  - ❖ optional extra vinyl circles (approx. 300mm) (see diag. #1)
- 'Happy Feet' mascot of your choice

11

RULES OF GAME:

- Players are shown the secret path by 'leader-in-charge' (see diag. #1)
- Player #1 attempts to repeat the steps of the secret path as they carry the 'Happy Feat' mascot with them.
- Each time they step onto a correct grid-space, the 'leader-in-charge' responds with "*Happy Feat!*" ... however if they step onto an incorrect grid-space then the 'leader-in-charge' responds with "*Not Happy Feat!*" At which point player #1 places the 'Happy Feat' mascot on the last correct grid-space and returns to the end of the line.
- Player #2 then begins and attempts to copy-step the secret path and pick up the 'Happy Feat' mascot so as to continue discovering the secret path.
- Play continues this way until the 'Happy Feat' mascot makes it safely across the grid with as many players as possible or until everyone has had 3 attempts across.
- This activity can be played by individuals, pairs or teams.

11

DESIGN & LAYOUT:

- Make up your own secret path ('X').
- Design your own obstacle course grid.
- By changing sides (north-south-east-west) each time you start a new game, it is possible to play many times with just the one secret path, as the grid looks quite different from each side.
- You can also reverse the direction of the same path, or mirror image it to give extra combinations with just the one path. Laminate your secret path for safe keeping & use.

Grid size = approx. 2100mm x 2100mm

11

diag #1

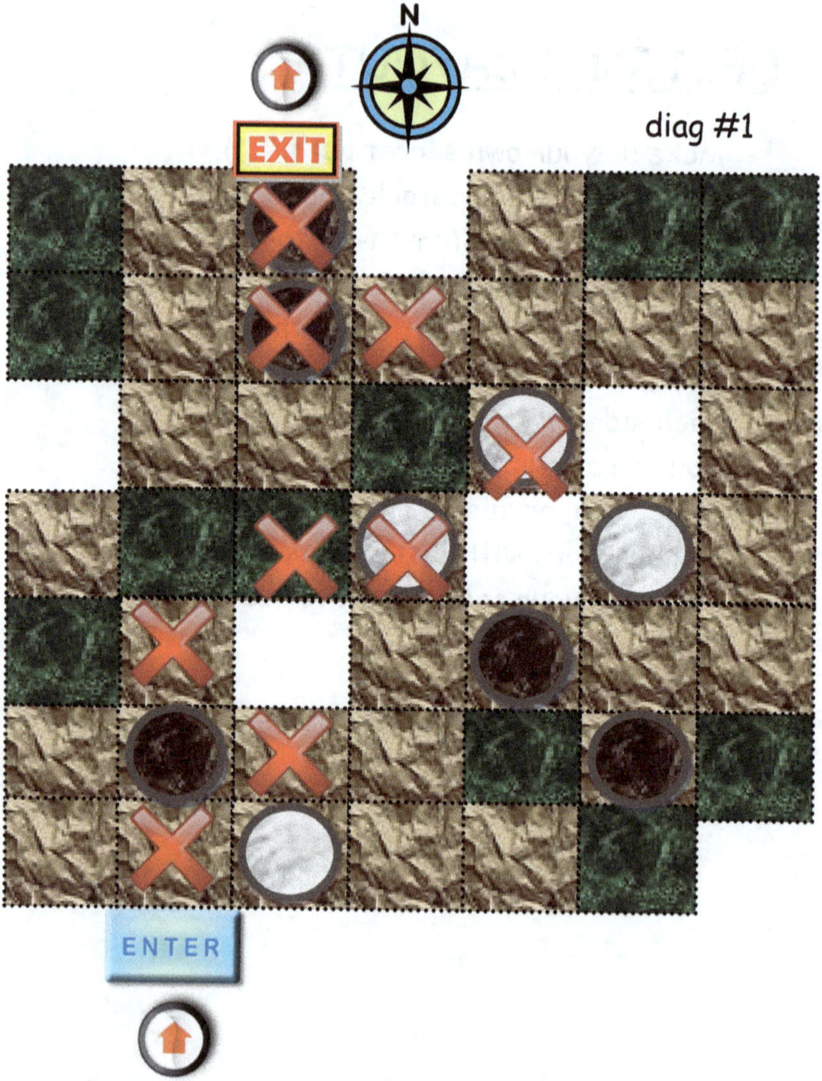

ENTER

NOTE: you can use any object as your Happy Feat Mascot...a clown, a penguin, or any other soft toy.

Happy Feat © Gary B Lewis 2012, 2022

12

SPOT ON
A competitive game of chance & skill for 2 – 4 players

AIM OF GAME:

- **To earn points by throwing rubber discs onto the grid. Winner scores the most points.**

EQUIPMENT REQUIRED:

- A grid of 16 squares (4x4) (See diag1. #1)
    - ❖ small carpet / mat squares (approx. 300mm square)
    - ❖ vinyl circles (approx. 200mm diameter)
    - ❖ chalk
- 24 small rubbers / plastic / wooden discs
    - ❖ (approx. 60mm diam./ approx. 5mm thick)
    - ❖ (6 of each colour)

Spot On © Gary B Lewis 2012, 2022

12

RULES OF GAME/HOW TO PLAY:

Players take turns to throw their discs one-at-a-time. They stand behind the line to throw. The line is approximately 900mm away for the nearest grid-spot. (See diag. #1)

Whenever a disc lands on a grid-spot it scores that player different points. (See diag. #1)

If a player's disc lands on the same grid-spot as another player's disc, then the first player's disc is removed from the game and their points for that space are deducted.

If a player lands on the same grid-spot as themselves they are safe and both discs score the same points. Players cannot try for 10pt or 20pt grid-spots unless they have 2 discs somewhere on the 1-5pts grid-spots

At the end of the game i.e. when all players have thrown all their discs, the scores are added up according to their grid-spots.

** For added interest a 'mystery grid-spot'

12

(worth 50 points) can be designated at the start of each new game, and only revealed at the end of that game.

LAYOUT (suggested):

Grid size = approx. 1200mm x 1200mm

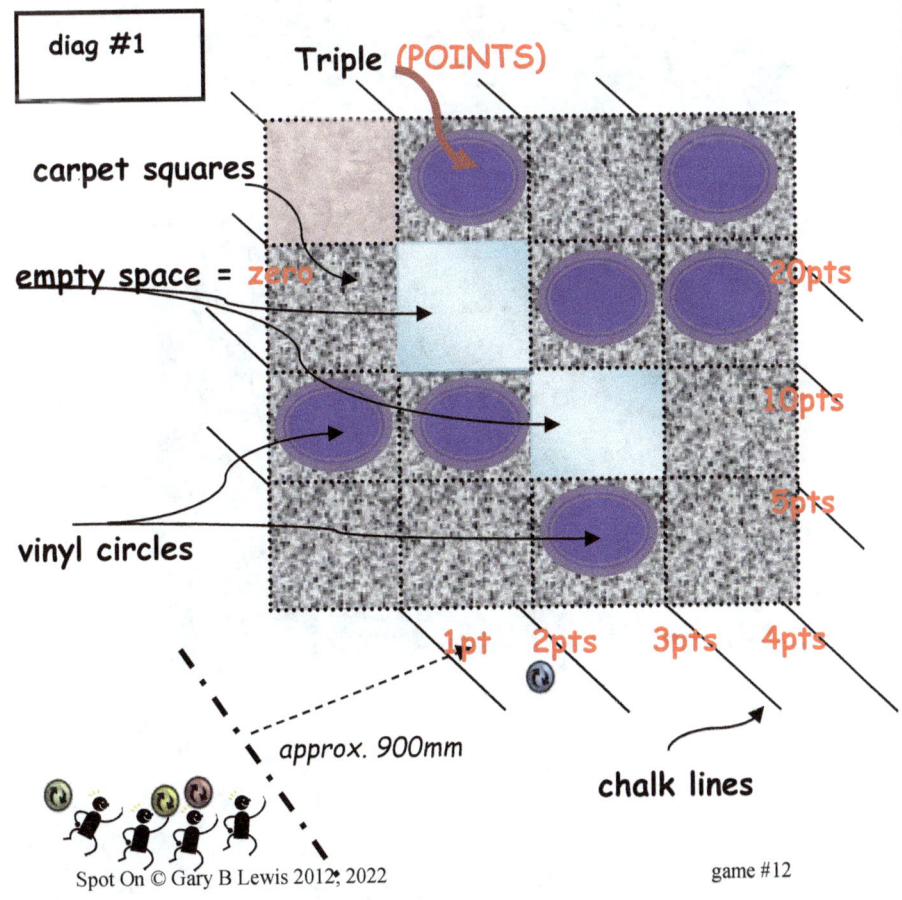

game #12

12

Spot On © Gary B Lewis 2012, 2022

game #12

#13

AIM OF GAME:

The aim of 'CHOPSTICK SUEY' ('TONGS OF NOODLES') is to score as many points as possible by picking up NOODLE BITS from one container — using giant chopsticks — and transferring them to another.

MATERIALS REQUIRED:

This game makes use of the 60 NOODLE BITS used in the game of 'KEBAB NOODLES' (see photos #1a & b)

- Make 3 different sized sets of chopsticks from approx. 300mm, 500mm & 600mm in length

#13

- use dowel or bamboo garden stakes, masking tape & thin plastic tubing (see photo #2)
- 1 x plastic tub / bucket round or square [NOODLE TUB]
- 1 x smaller tub container
- Chalk
- Stopwatch
- About 60 NOODLE BITS cut to varying thickness of between 10mm to 20mm. NOODLE BITS are the foam noodles used in swimming pools bought from $2.00 plus variety stores. They can be easily cut with a sharp breadknife.

photo #1a

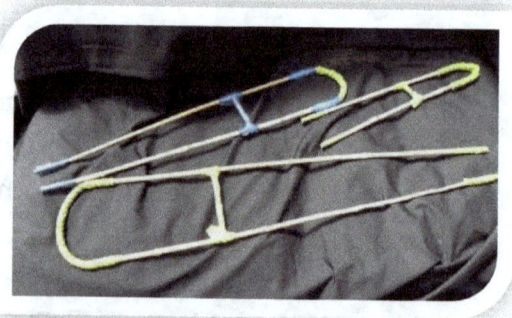

photo #2

photo #1b

Chopstick Suey © Gary B Lewis 2012, 2022

#13

LAYOUT:

- Place NOODLE TUB and empty TRANSFER tub anywhere between 300mm to 600mm – depending on the age and skill of the players
- Outline the playing area with chalk — allow a '<u>safe players</u>' area of somewhere between 300mm to 450mm

HOW TO PLAY:

The player selects which set of tongs they wish to use.

If they choose the larger sets they get a bit more time allocated i.e. the smallest set of tongs gets the least amount of time allocated. Suggested time allocations:

Chopstick Suey © Gary B Lewis 2012, 2022

#13

- Smallest set = 60 seconds
- Medium set = 75 seconds
- Large set = 90 seconds

They may use two hands with the tongs but must not touch any NOODLE BITS with their hands. If they drop a NOODLE BIT they can pick it up with their tongs but not their hand.

In the given time limit they have to try to pick up and transfer as many NOODLE BITS as they can from the NOODLE TUB into the spare tub / bucket. You can also limit the game by having them pick up one NOODLE BIT at a time or speed up the game by allowing more than one at a time.

#13

At the end of the time limit they count all the NOODLE BITS back into the main tub. As an option — and for intrigue — you could reveal a mystery colour score which would score them more points. E.g. if they transferred 22 NOODLE BITS — 5 of which were red, and the mystery colour revealed was red, then they could add another 25 points (5 bonus points per red NOODLE BIT) onto their score, thus giving them a score of 47.

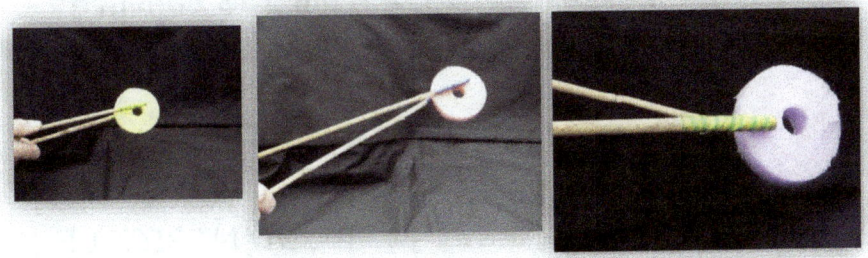

This game is also a great leveller in terms of the boastful, proud or arrogant student who thinks they are just 'so good' and that this game is 'so easy'. It is not as easy as it looks!

#14

AIM OF GAME:

The aim of 'KEBAB NOODLES' / 'HUNTERS & GATHERERS' is to score as many points as possible by skewering as many NOODLE BITS from the common tub in the middle.

MATERIALS REQUIRED:

This game makes use of 4 of the GIANT PICK-UP STICKS from Courtyard Games Book 1. (See book 1 for how to make)

- 4 coloured sticks approx. 600 mm in length – 1 x 4 colours

#14

- use dowel or bamboo garden stakes
- as a safety pre-caution position rubber stoppers on the ends
- 8 coloured arm bands to identify players
- 1 x square plastic storage tub
- About 60 NOODLE BITS cut to varying thicknesses of between 10mm to 20mm. NOODLE BITS are the foam noodles used in swimming pools bought from $2.00 plus variety stores. They can be easily cut with a sharp breadknife.
- Chalk
- stopwatch
- 4 carpet squares
- An area of approximately 4x4 metres i.e. 16 sq m

LAYOUT:

- Set up the tub, and mats as shown in diag. #1
- Outline the playing area with chalk and 4 stations
- One partner is the "HOLD & LOCK" or "STAY-AT-HOME PERSON" and the other is the "HUNTER-GATHERER- RUNNER"

#14

HOW TO PLAY:

Establish who will STAY-AT-HOME and who will be the HUNTER-GATHERER.

The STAY-AT-HOME must have one foot behind the mat and the other on the mat at all times (unless they have to rescue a NOODLE BIT that has come off their skewer).

SAFETY RULE:

STAY-AT-HOME player must hold their skewer horizontally across the front of their body during the game. The skewer should not be pointed up or out towards the running player.

The HUNTER-GATHERER player is to collect as many NOODLE BITS as possible – **ONE-AT-A-TIME** from the common tub in the middle of the playing area.

Kebab Noodles / Hunters & Gatherers © Gary B Lewis 2012, 2022 game #14

#14

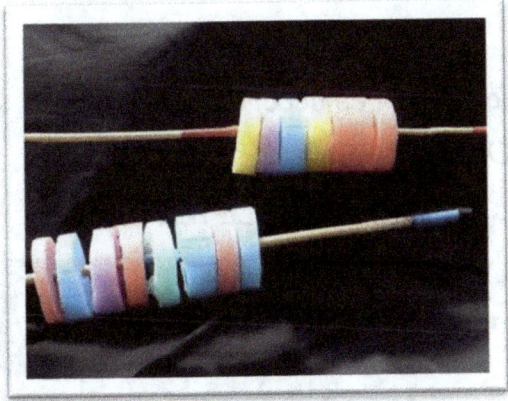

Each time the HUNTER-GATHERERS collect their NOODLE BIT they race back to where their STAY-AT-HOME partner is and place their NOODLE BIT on the skewer held by their partner.

Each time they place a NOODLE BIT on the skewer, they too must also have one foot on the mat.

The time limit is 1 minute for each round of play. After the scores for the round have been confirmed then the players swap positions so that the STAY-AT-HOME player now becomes the HUNTER-GATHERER and vice versa.

Kebab Noodles / Hunters & Gatherers © Gary B Lewis 2012, 2022

#14

SCORING:

1. Add up each team's scores according to the number of NOODLE BITS on their skewer.
2. Add on 5 points for each NOODLE BIT they have that matches their colour band.

3. Add on 10 points for each of the mystery colour NOODLE BITS … revealed from the organiser's pocket.

Kids love the intrigue of this game because the final score & winner is not always known until the mystery colour bonus points have been included.

#14

diag. #1

game #14

Kebab Noodles / Hunters & Gatherers © Gary B Lewis 2012, 2022

15

A team game for 4 - 12 players.

AIM OF GAME:

- To work as a team to get as many 'elephant snot balls' (tennis balls) down the elephant's trunk (air-con / concertina tubing) as possible within the given time-limit.

*In certain cultures this term may be offensive, so please be sensitive to the beliefs and customs of the children with whom you may find yourself working with. Please accept my sincere apology if any offence is taken. The title for this game came about as a spontaneous response from children and teachers when the game was first introduced. As I have essentially chosen to use this title within an Australian context; my suggested alternative name for the game is **'Squishy Tunnel'**.

15

EQUIPMENT REQUIRED:

- 25 tennis balls
- An off-cut of concertina tubing (air conditioning tubing) about 3 metres in length for the trunk
- 4 carpet squares (or chalked squares)
- Two containers – one at start for holding the balls and the other at the end to collect the 'snot balls'
- A timer / stop watch

15

DESIGN & LAYOUT:

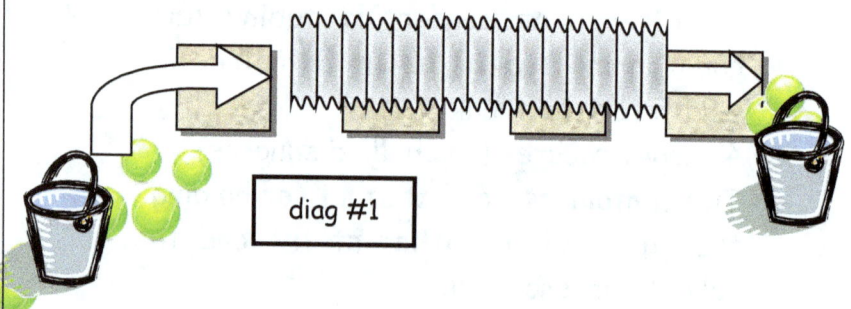

diag #1

HOW TO PLAY:

- Set up playing area as shown in (diag. #1)
- Players position themselves onto their designated positions e.g. diag. #1
    - player #1 would be at the start throwing balls through the trunk
    - players #2 & #3 would be at the second and third positions holding the trunk (tubing) in the best position for getting the balls through

NOTE: the more players on the team ...the more 'holding trunk' positions will be required

Elephant Snot © Gary B Lewis 2012, 2022

- player #4 is at the end collecting the 'snot balls' that come though into their bucket

- Each player should be given one minute at each position so that they all get a turn at throwing, holding & catching. So for the example in diag. #1, the team would be given overall 4 minutes.
    - *Suggest that you stop at the end of each minute to calculate the number of 'snot balls' caught, replace all the balls to the start, and each player repositions to their new place.*
    - *More advanced players can handle the total time allocation without breaking to change positions as long as you call out "change" at the end of each minute. This certainly adds for a much faster and chaotic game.*
    - *If player #1 uses all their balls they must call out "**Refill**" so that the last player can empty their bucket back into the first bucket.*

15

- Balls that fall onto the ground instead of into the catching bucket must be returned to the start bucket and not counted as 'snot balls' caught. Other children standing around watching (not-yet-playing) are always more than happy to assist by chasing the run-away 'snot balls'.

- In hot weather you could even have the first bucket partly filled with water — makes for a fun & refreshing activity.

* Children love to be competitive, and may be keen to compete as team against team. If you have access to more than one length of tubing and enough tennis balls you could have 'elephant' teams going head-to-head; otherwise just keep track of scores as you go.

    - *NOTE: world record score as of Dec 2011 is 245 'snot balls' caught within 4 minutes by a team of 4 students.*

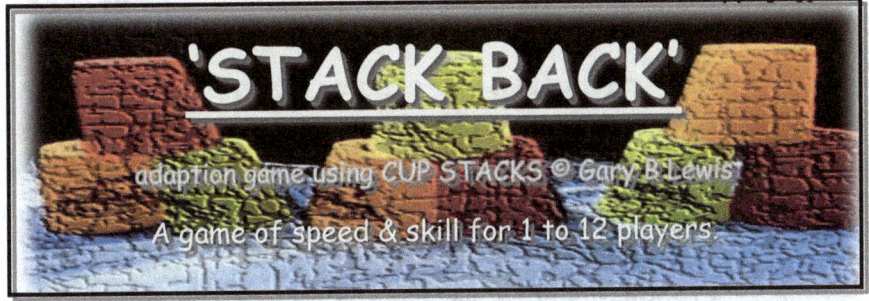

AIM OF GAME:

The aim of 'STACK BACK' is to beat your own time to re-arrange the CUP STACKS in the right order within a time limit ... or to beat your opponent.

MATERIALS REQUIRED:

- This game makes use of some SPEED STAX / CUP STACKS mentioned in Courtyard Games Book 1. http://courtyardgames.blogspot.com/

  SPEED STAX / CUP STACKS can be bought in certain toy stores or on-line. Just search for them through your search engine.

- Because you won't be using these cups for regulation SPEED STAX CUP STACKING, you

#16

can actually use any regular sized plastic cups — but they may stick unless you carefully drill holes in the bottom.

- You can use rubber play mats that come with standard SPEED STAX or you can use simply use carpet squares - this is essentially to reduce the noise factor if you are indoors. Outdoors shouldn't be a problem.

- You may also want to use tables or trestles, but not necessarily — the floor would do just as well.

- You will need to print out (& enlarge) copies of the STACK BACK PATTERN CARDS (laminate them if possible for durability.)

- A stopwatch / timer

- Enough cups for the number of players you intend to have playing e.g.

  - 1 player = 9 cups (3x3 colours) see photo #1
  - 2 players = 18 cups (3x3 colours each)
  - 3 players = 27 cups (3x3 colours each) etc

Stack Back © Gary B Lewis 2012, 2022

#16

diag #1

LAYOUT:

- Have the cups stacked into separate single stacks for each individual player e.g. as per diag. #1 each player would start off with a stack something like this in diag. #2

diag. #2

HOW TO PLAY

You can have the players set up side-by-side or head-to-head or randomly placed wherever you wish.

When the players are set and ready in place,

#16

present them with the STACK BACK PATTERN CARD (see pattern set below). You can either have one large, laminated card for all players to see or several individual small sized cards for each player to use or share between two. However, they do need to be *'reading off the same page'* so to speak.

On the word 'READY STACK GO' they are racing to unstack their cups and re-arrange them back into the STACK BACK PATTERN — hand in the air indicate 'finished'.

If playing with more than one player - fastest time wins. You can decide whether you play elimination rounds or best of 5 - however you choose to organize.

You can even build up the excitement towards a head-to-head championship game over a period of a few days /weeks.

This game is simply an exciting variation for those familiar with regular CUP STACKING, plus it will help those children who are less coordinated and less confident developmently.

#16

STACK BACK PATTERN CARDS

- On the next two pages you will find stencil patterns for making up your set of STACK BACK PATTERN CARDS.

- The colours used in the STACK BACK PATTERN CARDS cover a very wide range of combinations, but are in no way exhaustive. Feel free to develop your own combinations.

- The colours used are 3 of the basic colours available. Again you can vary the colours.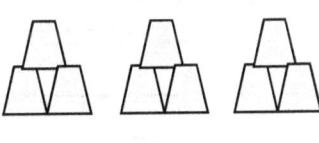

- Included is a blank set of STACK BACK PATTERN CARDS for you to colour according to the cups you have available.

- If you are adventurous you could even make you own 3X6 STACK BACK patterns.

Stack Back © Gary B Lewis 2012, 2022   game #16

#16

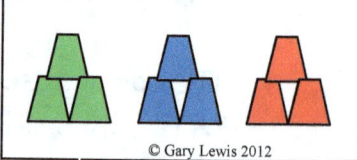

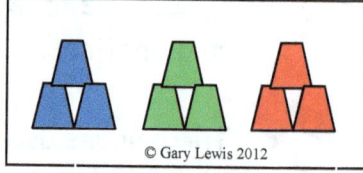

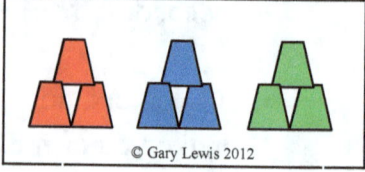

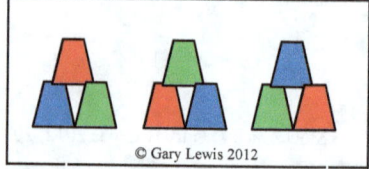

#16

#17

AIM OF GAME:

The aim of 'CATERPILLAR DERBY' / 'HEAD FIRST' is to get your caterpillar across the finish line – *head first!*

MATERIALS REQUIRED:

This game makes use of some of the pots and bowls from Courtyard Games Book 1.

- 4 sets of bowls – plus one additional pot to act as the head of the caterpillar (see photos #1a & b)

#17

- You can use any set of bowls, pots or markers as long as you have one that is different enough to be identified as the head
- The set used in photos #1a & b just happens to lock together the large pot into the smaller bowl – a lucky discovery & all on the cheap!
- 4 coloured arm bands to identify players
- Two large rubber dice inside a clear plastic container with a fixed lid — purchase these from any of $2 variety stores. (*Believe me this will save a lot of frustration and time.*)
- Chalk / masking tape
- An area of approximately 3x3 metres i.e. 9 sq m can be larger if you wish

Photos #1a & b

#17

LAYOUT:

- Draw or masking tape the race course however you want
- Set up the 'caterpillars' as shown in diag. #1
- Outline the playing area with chalk — clearly marking the start & finish and the walled barriers.

HOW TO PLAY:

Starting with the outside rail caterpillar – the player rolls the dice in the container, totals the score then moves their caterpillar forward – *starting from the back to the front.*

- This is done by taking the last bowl (tail) and jumping it over to the front – making sure that it is touching the head. If say they score 3+2 = 5, then they jump over the caterpillar body-parts 5 times (see diags #2a & b)

Caterpillar Derby © Gary B Lewis 2012, 2022

- If they wish to turn a corner – as in going around someone or around the 'bendy' shape of the racetrack, then all they do is to slightly place the front bowl (body part) to the side and make a new direction (see diag #2b)

Start the game relatively slowly so that each player has plenty of time to get their caterpillar into the game.

Play continues with each player taking turns in rolling the boxed dice and jumping their caterpillars around the race track.

Once all caterpillars are in the race, then speed up the pace of rolling, jumping and passing the dice. *The kids will love it when the game picks up speed to a chaotic gallop!*

The winner has to have their 'caterpillar's head' across the finish line - not just a body-part. Kids will be keen to all finish the game, to see who comes in 2nd, 3rd & 4th place.

#17

Re-set the caterpillars back at the start ready for the next game.

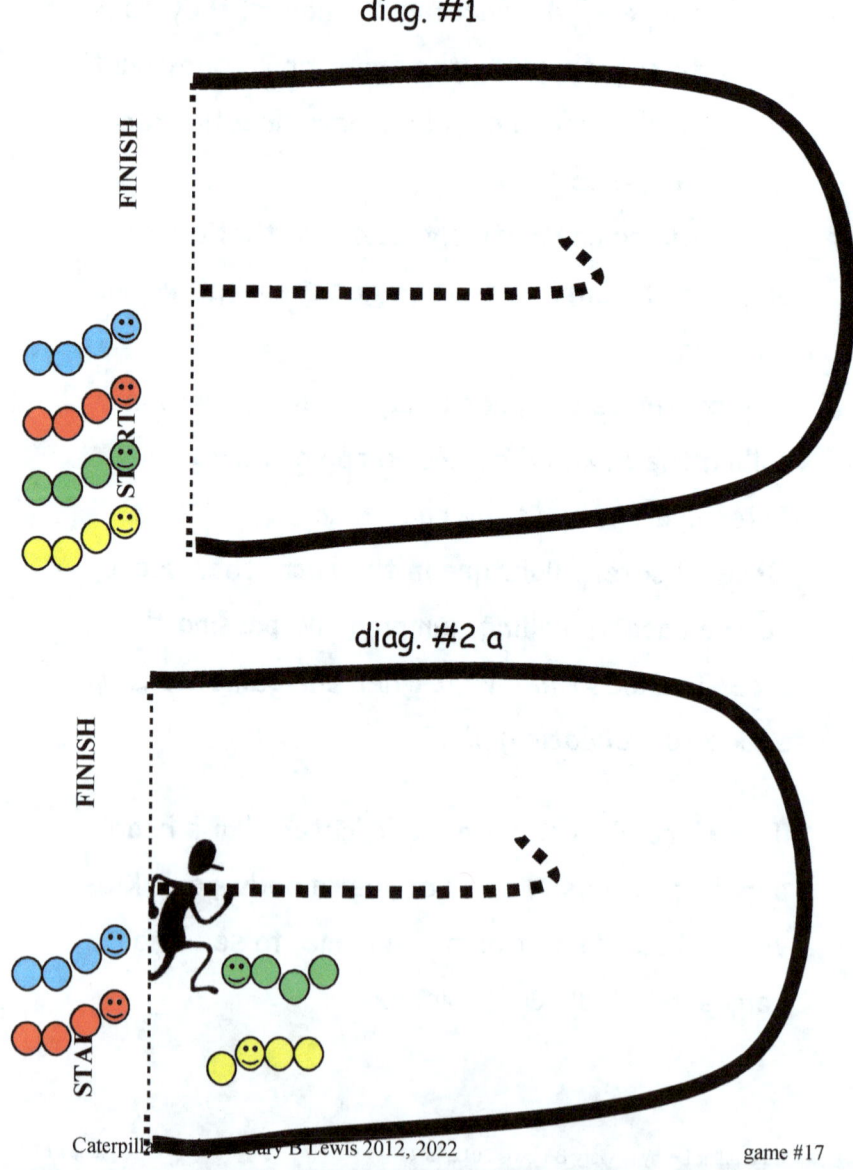

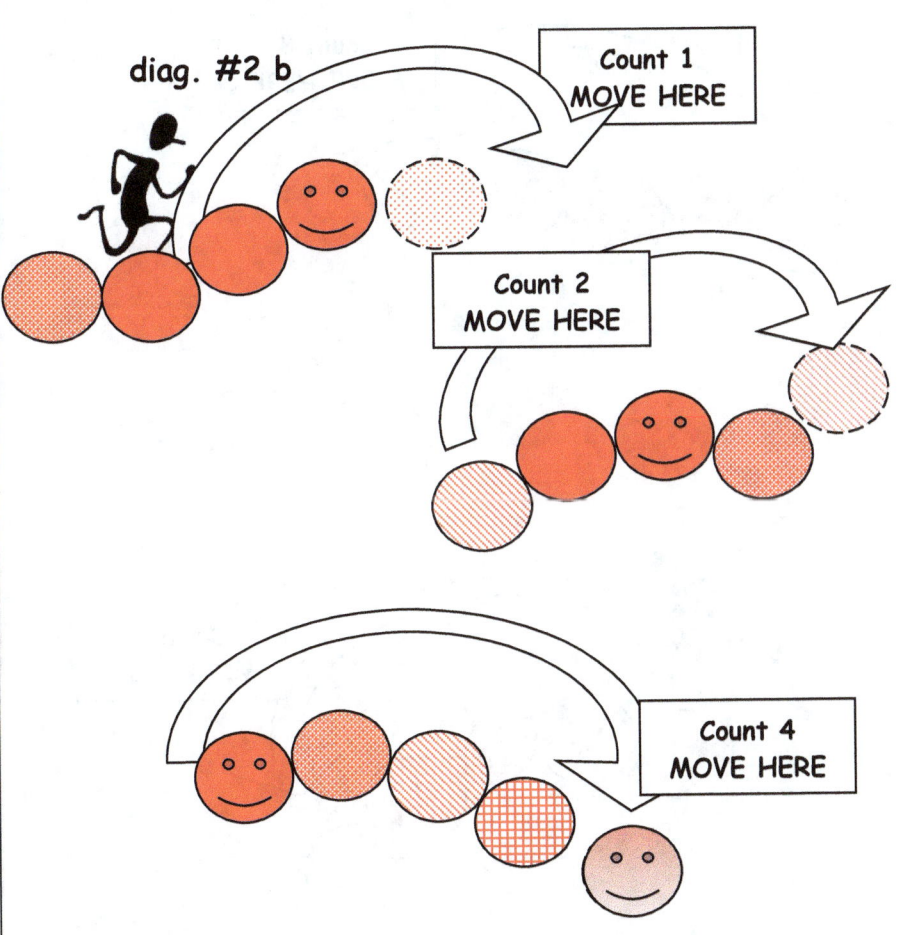

#17

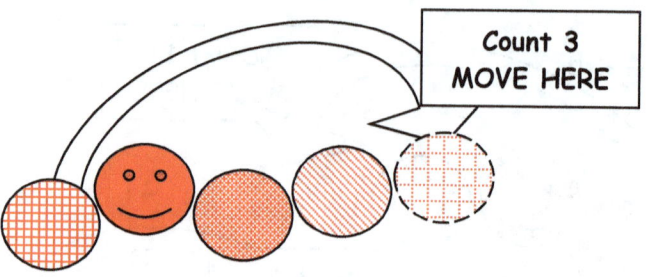

Caterpillar Derby © Gary B Lewis 2012, 2022

18

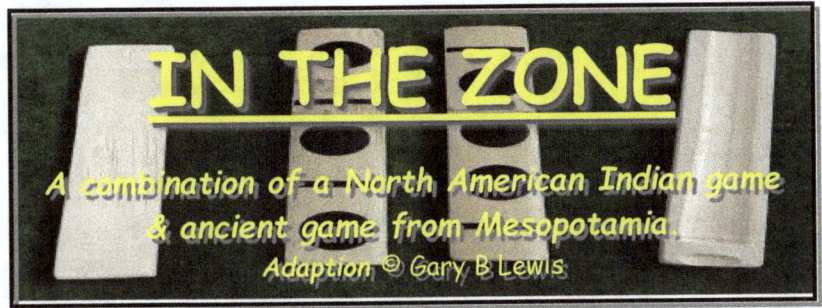

AIM OF GAME:

To get all 5 'markers' through the ZONE — in, around and off the playing board before your opponent

EQUIPMENT REQUIRED:

- grid-layout (see diag. #1) can be chalk drawn or carpet squares (approx. 300mm) and vinyl circles (approx. 300mm)
- 10 rubber or plastic markers / discs / cones (2 colours / 5 each)
- 5 STICK-DICE** made of large pop sticks (tongue depressors) or larger if you want to make your own – approx. 150mm x 30mm from thin MDF, plywood or off-cuts of bamboo

18

- Paint or draw pattern on one side of each stick (see photo #1)

DESIGN & LAYOUT:

diag. #1

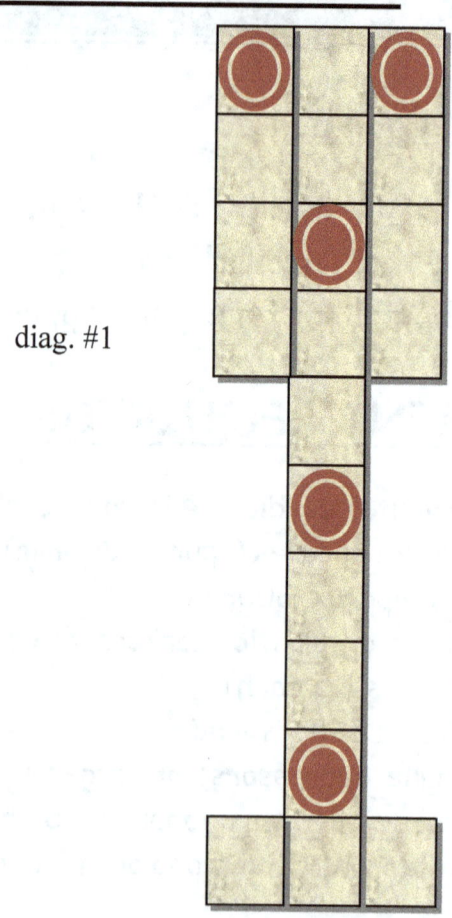

In the Zone © Gary B Lewis 2012, 2022

game #18

18

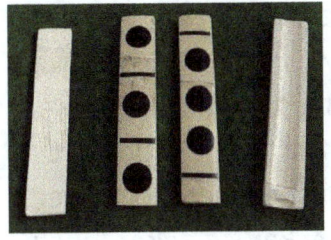

** STICK-DICE refers to the term given to dice throwing equipment used in various Native North American Indian games

photo #1

HOW TO PLAY:

- Set up playing grid as shown in (diag. #1)
- Players take turns to throw STICK-DICE – needing a "1", "2", "3" or "4" to enter (refer to photo #2a for scoring with STICK-DICE)

   *NOTE: You can use conventional dice if you wish (refer to **Caterpillar Derby & Domino Dice Down**) for details of using large rubber dice*

- Player can only enter at the entry points
- A player whose 'marker' lands on a 'safety-free zone' can either choose to stay safe from capture or have a free turn (diag. #2).
  - If the player chooses to have a free turn and lands on another

18

'safety-free zone' ... they cannot choose safety ... they must have another free turn immediately

- A player landing on the same space as opponent 'captures' their opponent's marker
  - A captured 'marker' is taken back to the start of the game
- A player can move any of their 'markers' in any order they choose

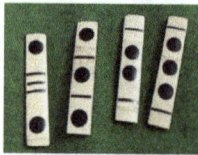 = 5 points

 points = 4

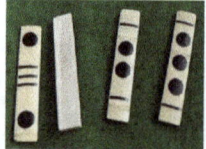 = 1 point

 = 2 points

 = 3 points

photo #1a

NOTE: DOTS & MARKS on stick dice are only decorative.!!! Scoring is as shown.
- 4 blank sides up = 4 points.
- 4 marked sides up = 5 points
- 1 blank & 3 marked = 1 point
- 2 blank & 2 marked = 2 points
- 3 blank & 1 marked = 3 points

In the Zone © Gary B Lewis 2012, 2022

game #18

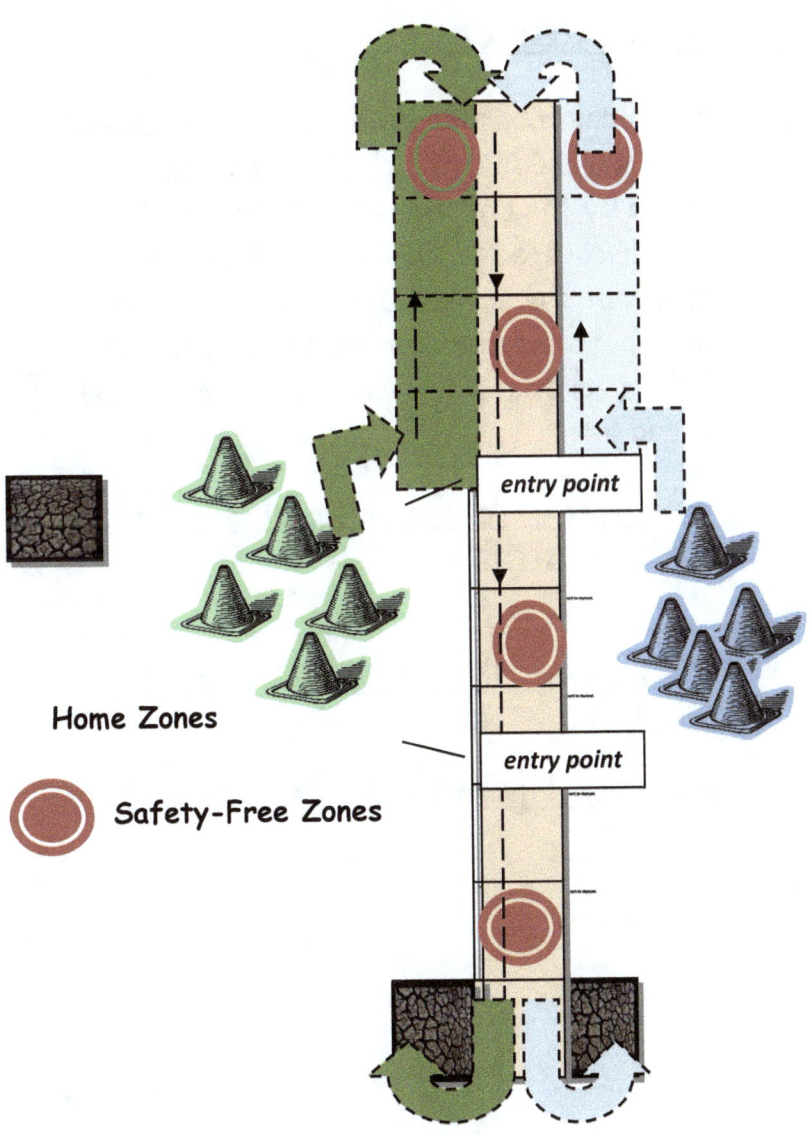

18

Historical aspects:

- The oldest board game has become known as "The Royal Game of Ur" or more commonly called by the Egyptians as "20 Squares". It was discovered in 1927 inside the Royal tombs of the ancient Sumerian city of Ur in Mesopotamia. The city was built more than 5000 years ago. Further information can be found at:

    http://www.iranica.com/articles/board-games-in-pre-islamic-persia

    http://www.mastersgames.com/rules/royal-ur-rules.htm

    http://www.ethnoludie.com/rules/ur/p04_en.html

18

STICK DICE

The Pomo Indians of California known for their finely polished beads for trade and their creation of an elaborate numbering and arithmetic system. The Pomo nation is also well known for their intricate basket weaving patterns which they also used to create the varied designs used on the stick dice. The stick-dice were made of wood were and either burnt etching or painted.

Further information can be found at:
http://mathcentral.uregina.ca/RR/database/RR.09.00/treptau1/game2.html

http://www.statemuseum.arizona.edu/activities/geents/index.shtml

http://hearstmuseum.berkeley.edu/exhibitions/ncc/gallery_3_5_5.html

#19

AIM OF GAME:

The aim of 'CODE BREAKER' is to break your opponent's secret number code before they break yours.

If you have kids who like to play 'GO-FISH' then they will love 'CODE BREAKER'!!

MATERIALS REQUIRED:

- 5 STICK-DICE** made of large pop sticks (tongue depressors) or larger if you want to make your own – approx. 150mm x 30mm

#19

from thin MDF, plywood or off-cuts of bamboo
- Paint or pattern on one side of each stick (see photos #1a & b)
- Alternatively you can use 1 large rubber die (dice) in a plastic container
* A stopwatch / timer (optional)
* 2 clipboards, blank or gridded paper
* 2 pencils / markers
* 30 sticks or pebbles or similar as their BANK VOLT

photo #1a

photo #1b

** traditionally STICK DICE games only use 5 sticks

#19

LAYOUT:

- There is no actual layout for this game (except for the gridded code sheets – see diag. #1) as it based on an interaction between two players - they can be standing or sitting
- This game can be played anywhere inside or outside
- It can be played by multiples of players (in pairs) at the same time – with smaller dice
- It could also be played in the car with smaller dice

daig. #1

	CODE #1	CODE #2	CODE #3	CODE #4	CODE #5	CODE TOTAL	NUMBER TO RISK
GAME #1	5	3	2	2	1	<u>13</u>	<u>17</u>
GAME #2							
GAME #3							

Code Breaker © Gary B Lewis 2012, 2022

#19

HOW TO PLAY:

- Each player determines their 5 DIGIT secret code and writes it on their gridded sheet in the relevant game section (see daig. #1).

    > NOTE: This page remains hidden for the entire game until their code is broken or the time limit is up.

- They then add up the total of their 5 DIGIT secret code then **reveal only the number left i.e. how many they are able to risk** [e.g. total of secret code = 13 ... able to risk = 17]
- Decide who will roll first.
    - If you are using the stick dice see photos below for reading

    (also **NOTE** on next page)

 =5   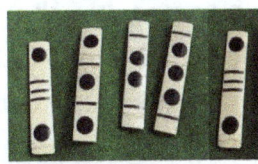 =6

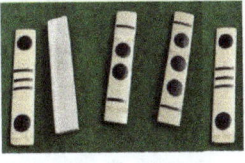 =1

Code Breaker © Gary B Lewis 2012, 2022

#19

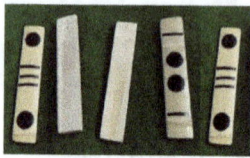 =2    =3

 =4

- Each time a player rolls the dice they can use that number to try to crack their opponent's SECRET CODE by saying "CODE 6" or "CODE 5" etc.
- If the guess of "CODE x?" reveals the first digit in the SECRET CODE then the guessing player is given that many sticks from their opponent's BANK VOLT.
- Then the other player has their roll of dice and challenges "CODE x?" and as per previous stage may also receive that many sticks from *their* opponent's BANK VOLT
    - If their guess is incorrect, then the guessing player must give their opponent the same number of sticks as per the guessed "CODE x?"
- A player can choose to not guess "CODE x?" e.g. with "NO CODE" and so both players

Code Breaker © Gary B Lewis 2012, 2022

#19

remain safe. However a player cannot guess "NO CODE" more than twice in a row.
- A player can have more than one of the same digits in their SECRET CODE
- If a player runs out of sticks in their BANK VOLT - they are out of the game
- The winner can be determined 3 ways:
    1. the player who cracks their opponent's SECRET CODE first
    2. or causes their opponent to reduce their BANK VOLT to the point that they can no longer pay out
    3. or the player with the most sticks in the BANK VOLT when the time limit is up e.g. after 5 mins (predetermine the time before the game begins)

> **NOTE: DOTS & MARKS on stick dice are only decorative.!!!**
> **Scoring is as shown.**
> - 5 blank sides up = 6 points.
> - 5 marked sides up = 5 points
> - 1 blank & 4 marked = 1 point
> - 2 blank & 3 marked = 2 points
> - 3 blank & 2 marked = 3 points
> - 4 blank & 1 marked = 4 points

#20

DOMINO DICE DOWN*

Original adaption © Gary B Lewis

A strategy / chance game for 3 or 4 players. *

A variation of Domino Dice Elimination Book 1

AIM OF GAME:

To cover as many domino boards with your marker, by rolling dice and adding numbers shown. **Winner** has the most number of markers down or disposes of all their markers.

MATERIALS REQUIRED:

- MDF cut outs with foam / painted circles (see photo #1)
- 27 pieces approx. 225mm x 600mm (smaller size to suit your needs)

#20

Make use of all combinations from **1** to **12** e.g.
'**1**' = 0/1; '**2**' = 0/2 & 1/1; '**3**' = 0/3 & 1/2;
'**4**' = 0/4, 1/3 & 2/2 ... etc up to '**12**' = 6/6

(include all doubles ***except for double zero***)

Photo #1

24 markers
    4 players 6 x 4 colour markers
    3 players 8 x 3 colour markers
    2 players 12 x 2 colour markers

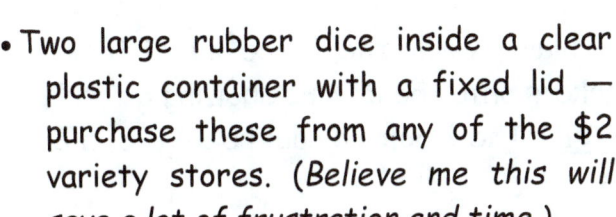

- Two large rubber dice inside a clear plastic container with a fixed lid — purchase these from any of the $2 variety stores. (*Believe me this will save a lot of frustration and time.*)

LAYOUT:

My suggestion is to set out the dominoes end-on-end on the ground in a large rectangle/square—in no particular order—and have all the action of play inside the square. This also helps to separate players

#20

from on-lookers, by restricting the inside to players only.

HOW TO PLAY:

Player rolls dice by shaking the container *(this makes a great noise ... half the fun!)* which is Photo #2

Then they add the numbers to get a score for example see (see photo #3) in the above case — a score of 7. In order to save time, it is best for the facilitator to call out the numbers and the total, to assist the player in their quest to find the correct total domino.

The player would then place one of their markers onto the domino showing a total of 7. <u>NOTE</u>: The 7 domino could be 4 & 3, 5 & 2 or 6 & 1.

If their domino score has been covered with a marker already, then they should quickly re-calculate before their next turn, and look for another domino. If they discover no domino available then they forfeit being able to place a marker for that turn.

#20

Starting the game slowly works best - particularly for younger children, and then once everyone has had a turn, increase the speed of dice rolling, which adds to the excitement.

Play continues until one player has placed all their markers down (everyone should have one more turn following the announcement of the first one finished). Players then go and collect & count how many of their markers are down on dominoes.

'GIANT DOMINOES' & 'DOMINO DICE ELIMINATION' games in

COURTYARD GAMES (BOOK 1)

http://courtyardgames.blogspot.com/

Check out
COURT YARD GAMES BOOK 1

http://courtyardgames.blogspot.com/

www.ingramcontent.com/pod-product-compliance
Lightning Source LLC
Chambersburg PA
CBHW050317010526
44107CB00055B/2288